FOUR LITTLE LINDSAYS

Also by Jeanne Warren Lindsay
(Partial listing)

The *P.A.R.E.N.T. Approach*

Your Baby's First Year

El primer año de tu bebé

The Challenge of Toddlers

El reto de los párvulos

Teen Dads: Rights, Responsibilities and Joys

Papás Adolescentes

Teenage Couples — Expectations and Reality

Teenage Couples — Caring, Commitment and Change

Teenage Couples — Coping with Reality

Pregnant? Adoption Is an Option

Do I Have a Daddy? A Story for a Single-Parent Child

By Jeanne Lindsay and Jean Brunelli
Your Pregnancy and Newborn Journey

Tu embarazo y el nacimiento de tu bebé

Nurturing Your Newborn

Crianza del recién nacido

By Jeanne Lindsay and Sally McCullough
Discipline from Birth to Three

La disciplina hasta los tres años

By Jeanne Lindsay, Jean Brunelli, and Sally McCullough
Mommy, I'm Hungry!

¡Mami, tengo hambre!

Four Little Lindsays and How They Grew 1957-1959

By

Jeanne Warren Lindsay

Morning Glory Press

Buena Park, California

Library of Congress Cataloging-in-Publication Data
available upon request.

ISBN 978-1-932538-99-1

MORNING GLORY PRESS, INC.
6595 San Haroldo Way   Buena Park, CA 90620-3748
714.828.1998, 1.888.612.8254   FAX 714.828.2049
e-mail: info@morningglorypress.com
Web site: www.morningglorypress.com
Printed and bound in the United States of America

Contents

Preface

When I found letters I wrote to my dad in the 1950s, I decided to make copies, put them together in a little booklet, and give one to each of my five kids for Christmas. I figured they would enjoy knowing a little about their lives as preschoolers.

But I got carried away. I found more letters. I started thinking about the differences between rearing children fifty years ago and now. I kept photos through the years, but only in one decade were those photos organized and labeled with names and dates. And that decade was the 1950s. Obviously that little booklet needed a few photos.

My project grew. I realized other people rearing children in the 50s might be interested. Those who were children in the 50s may enjoy comparing how they were raised with the strategies they used with their own children. My project morphed into this book.

Acknowledgments

I'm especially grateful to Mike, Steve, Pati, Eric and Erin for making these stories possible. Several friends encouraged me to publish these letters, and in this way, share our lives. Ev Lerman wrote the Foreword, a wonderful boost for an author. Marilyn Reynolds, who writes superb novels for young adults, also encouraged me. Friends in my two Life Stories groups offered helpful suggestions.

Tim Rinker designed the cover. Carole Blum, Pati Lindsay, and Geri Lawson helped with the proofreading.

Most of all, I thank Bob, our children's wonderful father, who lived to see his children grown up. He was very proud of them and of our seven fabulous grandchildren. We all loved him.

Foreword

Jeanne Lindsay, my publisher, my editor, my friend who dragged me through two books on teen pregnancy prevention, was asking me to write a foreword for her latest book? I was filled with conflicting emotions – excitement, pride, fear, and most of all, surprise. She was turning the tables on me. In our relationship over the ten years we had known each other she had been the mentor, the editor, the guardian angel of my books, the publisher who brought them to life. She had even written the foreword to my first book.

I whipped through those emotions before choosing my initial instinct when confronted with a challenge. Of course I would, but she had to promise she'd turn it down if she didn't like it. Or at the very least, edit it until she did. Jeanne laughed and promptly sent me the manuscript.

I cancelled my life for the next few days, settling down to her description of a collection of letters she had written to her Dad when she was raising her children, starting with the time when four were under five years old. She told him she wanted him to know his grandchildren even though they lived far away from each other. She also, with her unvarnished honesty and warmest tact, told him that one day she hoped to write and this was a way of practicing. So I was prepared to get to know Jeanne's children whom I had never met, but I was not prepared to get to know the young Jeanne whom I also had never met.

Our first meeting was during a conference on teen pregnancy prevention, where I found her having lunch between presentations and manning her sales booth. I had just written *Teen Moms* and, looking for a publisher, was sent to see Jeanne by a mutual friend working as an advocate for teens.

The conference was on the East coast of Florida and I lived on the West coast, so I flew across, chased a taxi, and arrived just in time to spend half an hour with Jeanne. She was charming, warm, and a little surprised to be meeting me unannounced, but by the time we finished lunch she said, "Well, Ev, I don't know anything about your book or if I'll like it, but I do like you."

So began my love affair with Jeanne. We met again at conferences, at sales booths, at her home in California, at my home in Florida, and once memorably, at the 25th anniversary party of Morning Glory Press, the publishing house she started when she couldn't find a publisher for the book she was then writing on teen pregnancy and related problems. I thought I knew her, and I thought a book of letters about raising her children couldn't give me any new insights into this remarkable woman. But I was wrong.

I had expected to read about child rearing in the 50s and 60s, the years in which I was doing the same. I had expected to read about stay-at-home Moms and working Dads. I had expected to gain insights into Jeanne's perceptions of the mores, customs, values, and activities of the time. I had expected to see a sharp photograph of our culture during that period of transition after World War II.

It was all there, much of it in sharp detail, all through the eyes of a loving mother, devoted wife, good neighbor, charming hostess, and extraordinary friend. Jeannie detailed illnesses, sibling rivalries, major and minor catastrophes, delightful and loving moments in the family, picnics in February in Iowa, struggles to afford the necessities and the occasional frivolities of life, living in a community with other young families and their concerns, all told with Jeanne's humor and optimism that everything always turns out all right. So I got what I expected, but what I didn't expect, and by which I was overwhelmed and thrilled, was a portrait of my friend as a young woman struggling through society's expectations and her own natural, bubbling-over creativity, tamping it down in one place only to have it burst through in another.

The first signs of this struggle for identity were in Jeanne's descriptions of the special meals she created, all of which sounded terrible to me. I could picture her, having filled the needs of her children and her husband, having attended another boring, going-nowhere meeting of some committee or other, and finding herself with a spare hour. Never one to waste a minute, an idea, or a potential adventure, Jeannie decided to whip up something. Her descriptions of doubling something good in a recipe (not necessarily with good results), of combining unlikely ingredients, and her family's dutiful response, are wonderful.

Her views of child rearing, spanking especially, emerge as she grows, along with one child and then another, expanding the boundaries of the popular wisdom of the day, substituting her innate good judgment for what was expected of her. She broadens her views as each child presents different challenges, and decides that they will grow up almost in spite of her.

We see her growth again as she reaches out to different organizations, testing her administrative skills, her organizational skills, and her group management skills. She begins leaving her children with sitters, with friends, overnight with her husband Bob, always repaying their kindnesses with her bountiful good works, good baking, and good friendship. In between making her own clothes and some of the children's, she tucks in dolls' clothes, more I thought to satisfy her own creative juices than for her daughter.

She says of herself, "I'm not the brainy one in the family," so it's OK for her to be home and for Bob to be working, but as a reader I thought she did protest too much. In keeping with the mores of the times, she offers her Dad a separate bedroom for his friend Cleora, if they choose to visit. She had to chuckle over that when she reread the letter many years later, so stretched had her thinking become by her later work with teen mothers and their problems.

Jeanne's understanding of the needs of others, her husband and her children, her neighbors and her extended family, always led her to fulfill them before she fulfilled herself, but she found a way to do both when she went back to school to become a home economics teacher. As she describes herself reading for class while her youngest child, her bonus baby Erin, climbs all over her, she foretells her future role in life. She breastfeeds in church, quietly and appropriately, breaking down another barrier without making a sound. Later she will work with teen mothers breaking down barriers to their education, to their acceptance, and to their development.

There are wonderful moments in the letters when Jeannie talks about money at that time – she sold their house for $15,000 in 1959, she paid her baby sitter 35 cents an hour, but even then half a bottle of an antibiotic cost $4.50. Never did she complain that they had too little; she always found a way to make their lives work, even backing Bob in his quest for a sports car that didn't quite fit the family. She lived within the bounds of the possible, but always knew that there was the impossible just waiting to be reached.

The world gained an advocate for teens and a world-class publisher when Jeanne went into business. I gained a publisher and a friend. And in this book I gained an understanding of the young Jeanne as she was developing into the mature woman of talent, of grace, and of consequence. She had done a wonderful job of raising her children and now she was to become an advocate for children with a reach well beyond her own hearth.

To quote Wallace Stegner, a writer whom I greatly admire, "A writer must be the sort of a man from whom a masterpiece is possible." Jeanne is the sort of woman from whom a masterpiece in the art of living evolved.

Evelyn Lerman, Author
Teen Moms: The Pain and the Promise
Safer Sex: The New Morality

*Dedicated with great love
to Mike, Steve, Pati, Eric,
Bonus Baby Erin,
and to Bob's memory*

Pat, Eric, Mike, and Steve watch "Captain Kangaroo."

Introduction

In July 1957, my father, Will Warren, was alone out on his farm near Garnett, Kansas. My mother had died several years earlier, and my dad, 64 and used to his wife doing all the home-making tasks, didn't do well as a single person. My first baby was born the week my mother died, and by 1957, we had three more babies. We lived 350 miles away in West Des Moines, Iowa. Obviously I was not doing much to assuage Dad's loneliness.

I decided better communication might help, and I even had an ulterior motive for that communication. I wrote to Dad:

> *Now that Eric is a month old and life has calmed down a little, I plan to write to you more often. Since we're to-gether so seldom, I'll describe Mike, Steve, Pat, and Eric and their activities in some detail. I'd like you to feel you know them when we do get together.*
>
> *Another reason I plan to write in detail – although I don't want to take time to attempt free-lancing magazine articles now, I'd like to practice writing regularly. Twenty years from now if I want to free-lance, I'd rather not have*

to waste several years learning how. So perhaps I could
learn a little now in this way — I'll write you a letter
regularly telling you of the children's activities. I'll make a
carbon for my file, and send the original to you.

I never freelanced. My writing life took a different direction.
But I'm glad I kept carbons of those letters. (Remember carbons?
No computers then.) I'm also glad I found them recently. It's not
easy, around my home anyhow, to find things 50 years later!

We were living in a new development, a single row of houses,
each containing about 900 square feet of living space. Behind us
was a steep hill, a wonderful place for sledding during the
Iowa winters.

Beyond our yard, down at the bottom of the hill, was a huge
cornfield. That cornfield became an enormous development after
we left Iowa, block after block of houses and strip malls.

We had sidewalks in front of the houses, but instead of a
gutter, a big ditch, then the road. Children were absolutely not
to cross that ditch. Across the road was a cemetery populated
by two beautiful swans along with lots of graves. We frequently
took the children across to visit with the swans.

We were the fifth house from the corner. By 1957, 14 children
aged 10 and under, 12 of them under age 8, lived in those five
houses. When I wrote that first letter, Eric was a month old; Pat,
20 months; Steve, 39 months; and Mike, a month from his fifth
birthday. We had no fences except a six-foot long structure we
put up in the back on one side of our lot to give us a little
privacy.

Life in the suburbs, at least in West Des Moines, was very
different for the kids than it is today. There was a great deal of
freedom. They all, once they could navigate by themselves, had
the run of the neighborhood, at least the neighborhood behind
those first five houses. As they grew older, they traveled further
to play. No play dates then. Play dates weren't needed. One

simply played with whomever was handy – and a lot of play-mates were nearby.

To a surprising extent, siblings looked after the littler ones. In fact, the older children of the block (the 5-7-year-olds) often included the little ones in their play.

Parenting in the Fifties

Parenting in the 1950s was different. Compared to today, an amazing amount of freedom was deemed okay for the children. Parenting differed in other ways, too. In fact, with each generation, accepted practices of child rearing change significantly through the years.

My father was born in 1893. He wore dresses until he was 4 or 5 years old. Children were to be seen and not heard at that time. Almost all babies were breastfed throughout the first year. When they started eating table food, they ate what the adults ate.

By the time my husband and I were born in the late 1920s, bottle-feeding had become acceptable for many mothers. The federal publication on baby care for that time included instructions on toilet training one's baby when he was three months old. The mother was told to put the baby on the potty chair on her lap at that age and expect him to perform!

A few years before our children were born, the baby books sternly admonished Mom to feed the baby strictly on schedule. (Babies born with wristwatches?) For most babies, according to the book, this meant every four hours. If a baby couldn't cope with that schedule, then it was okay to switch to feeding him every three hours, but again, strictly by the clock. Apparently no baby needed a 31/2 hour schedule.

When our children were born, that schedule conviction still prevailed to quite an extent. I didn't exactly follow those instructions, but thought if I were an ideal mom, I "should" get each one on a schedule as quickly as possible.

In the 50s, breastfeeding was not typical, at least not among my friends. Bottles were still widely used. I chose to breastfeed, but had absolutely no guidance on how to do so successfully. And I was trying to put those babies on a four-hour schedule! Now I know that the stomachs of newborns can hold about one teaspoon of food, and therefore infants need to be fed frequently, actually every two or three hours during the first weeks, sometimes even more often. But I didn't know that in the 50s, and nobody suggested such a wild idea to me.

Back then, we were told to start feeding the baby solid food as early as possible, at least by two months. We know now that feeding solid food too early is likely to cause allergies for that baby as s/he grows older. Babies should stay away from solid food for at least four months, preferably six. In fact, the American Academy of Pediatrics now recommends that *all* babies be breastfed with no solid food for the first six months.

Our Steve has rather severe allergies, no doubt at least partly caused by my spooning cereal into his mouth when he was only a few weeks old. After all, I wanted to be a good mom, and we thought the best mom was the one who fed her baby solid food the earliest.

I really cringed when I read my proud statement that I had gained no weight in my last three months of pregnancy (page 76). I had already gained 18 pounds, and at that time, doctors considered 15-18 pounds weight gain ideal during pregnancy. So I dieted. Not a good way to go.

For my second pregnancy, the doctor even prescribed diet pills! Thank goodness the one or two I took made me feel so jittery, I threw the rest away. We know now that most women need to gain 25-35 pounds during pregnancy, and diet pills are an absolute no-no during this time.

My Changing Parenting Philosophy

Some of the things I read in these letters, strategies we used to discipline our children, I firmly disagree with now. I have refrained from adding editorial notes to the letters. I decided they would give a more honest picture of life at that time if left as written. However, as I read them now, sometimes I sigh deeply. I'm the author or co-author of a seven-book series on parenting, and some of my current thinking on appropriate parenting does *not* match our practices in the 50s.

We ran a pretty tight ship when we were parenting four children under five. We spanked occasionally for various misdeeds. I firmly believe now that spanking teaches a child that bigger people can hit little people, but not much else. A swat on a child's bottom is not likely to physically harm him, but neither is it likely to teach him to behave any better.

I think we finally learned that lesson by the time Erin, our Bonus Baby, was born. I'm quite sure we never spanked Erin. Or could it have been because she was practically an only child as she was growing up? Does the phenomenon of several small children tearing around and behaving as small children do more likely lead to spanking? Probably . . . which doesn't make it right.

As an example, on page 65, I write,

> *The other evening I heard Bob go in the bathroom, take Steve out of the tub, and spank him soundly. I asked later what had happened. He said Steve had a toy cup, and was nonchalantly pouring cups of water out of the tub onto the floor. Pat was standing there with a towel, mopping up as fast as he poured.*

Today I don't think I'd spank Steve for dumping water on the floor. After all, Pat was keeping it mopped up. On the other hand, we had wood floors, so soaking the bathroom floor with water wasn't such a good idea.

Insisting Steve clean up his mess seems a better approach – except he would probably have enjoyed the "punishment." But is that really a problem? The important thing was to teach him

Perfect Homemaker – 1950s Style
Written in 1957

Too many women sit around worrying because Pat isn't toilet-trained by her second birthday or because there's dust on the TV. Two of my friends have had nervous breakdowns lately, largely because of fruitless searches for perfection.

Of course this theory must be tempered with a liberal sprinkling of common sense. If I lose my temper with the children for a minor sin, I'll regret it, but I won't let it ruin our day. I don't want to behave as I did the first couple of years I had children. I read Dr. Spock, followed his advice whenever possible, and felt terrible when I slipped up. Feeling guilty, I discovered, is not the best attitude for a mother to have. Do your best, first of all, then cut worry down to a minimum.

A woman always feeling guilty about her homemaking can't possibly operate at peak efficiency. With all the wonderful things we do today (rear lots of children, participate in community activities, hold part- or full-time jobs, garden), it's a shame to waste effort fussing over our inadequacies, whether real or imagined.

The "perfect because she's not perfect" homemaker realizes that as her family changes, so do her homemaking standards. Before she had children, maybe she kept her house spic and span. Perhaps she spent several hours a day cooking intricate dishes. She served a term as president of her local political group.

But several years later when she has several pre-school children, she's perfectly willing to cut cleaning to a minimum (probably concentrating on picking up rather than cleaning up), and to prepare quick and easy, but good meals. She may continue to participate in a favorite organization, but cheerfully says "No, but ask me again in a few years" to other requests for help. She cuts down on these activities to make time for playing with her children as well as taking care of their physical needs.

Why feel guilty about "lowering" standards? Most children are away from home by the time their mothers are 45. The next 20 or 30 years will leave lots of time for outside activities.

Sure, I'm not a perfect homemaker. But I'm trying my damnedest not to worry about it.

not to dump water on the bathroom floor. Spanking was not a good solution.

As I think of those years when the children were small, my memories are mostly pretty positive. Of course I got tired and upset, and undoubtedly screamed at my kids, but by and large, we had a good time. Being able to stay home during that time was an important part of that satisfaction.

On the opposite page is an article I wrote in 1957. It illustrates the mind set of the times, I think. First, we were *homemakers,* a perfectly good term for then or now. Young parents today who work full time certainly are homemakers too. But in the 50s, there was a greater emphasis on the importance of "standards" in homemaking, i.e., that the home must be clean, the meals perfect, etc., even as many moms were caring simultaneously for several preschool children. These moms ideally were to stick with child-rearing until their children were grown, and be the perfect homemaker as they did so. Many of us thought this was the way it was supposed to be. My article was written in protest of that ideal.

I can remember actually thinking and talking with Bob about my philosophy of child rearing. True to my era, I thought ideally Mom would stay home with the kids while Dad earned the living. I also knew I was interested in a career. But instead of trying to do both, as so many young mothers must do today, I thought it best to focus on the parenting for a while.

I thought this was a reason to have several children. Parenting three or four (or six, our original plan) would make it "worthwhile" to stay home. I would find it a little hard to defend that conviction now. However, I still think, if Dad can earn the living and Mom can stay home with the children, *and* mom *wants* to be home, it can be a lovely way to live. But I no longer think this is the "way it's supposed to be" for everyone.

We are all so different, and we can parent well in different ways. We can't have, or should not have rules as to who cares for the children full-time. Really good day care can be an excellent substitute for full-time Mom care. And of course Dad might well be the one who stays home and parents the children.

I was shocked to read, 50 years later, my comment on page 77 about the woman who wanted to be a doctor. I read about her in the April 1958 *Ladies Home Journal* "How America Lives" story. Instead of going to medical school, this woman married young and quickly had several children. Then she realized she still wanted to be a doctor. She and her husband decided to make the necessary sacrifices for her to realize her dream. At the time the story was written, she was ready to begin practicing medicine and was convinced her husband, a factory worker, would quit his job and find another wherever she chose to practice.

My reaction to that story? No, I didn't admire the mother's ambition or how much it might mean to her children and her husband for her to realize her dream. Instead, I wrote, "The article was interesting, but sounded sort of awful, too. I'm glad I'm not the brainy one in this family. It's much more convenient when it's the man who is ambitious." Today, I would admire her for following her dream, knowing that she could also parent well, perhaps because she was also doing what she needed to do. I also finally realized that Bob and I had different interests and abilities, and that this did not mean one was "brainier" than the other.

Apparently I hadn't discovered Women's Liberation yet when these letters or the "Perfect Homemaker" article were written.

Actually, I think my generation of women were the lucky ones. So many of us stayed home to parent our kids while they were little, then had time for the careers we wanted. We had it both ways. For many young parents today, this is not possible.

Our parenting methods worked pretty well after all. After some very traumatic teen years, all five children are living satisfying lives. For a synopsis of Mike, Steve, Pati, Eric, and Bonus Baby Erin as adults, see the "Afterword."

PART I

1957
Four Under Five

All dressed up for church – Steve, Pat, Mike with Daddy (Bob).

July 3, 1957

Dear Dad,

Sunday we decided Eric mustn't be a heathen all his life — after all, he's a month old and had never been to church. So we put his new suit on him, got the rest of us ready, and all six of us took off. Bob took Eric in his basket, and set it in the crib at the church nursery. Pat was there to look after him. The woman in charge said he was the youngest ever left there during church.

Afterward, Bob could scarcely get to him, for half a dozen parents were grouped around him oohing and aahing about how

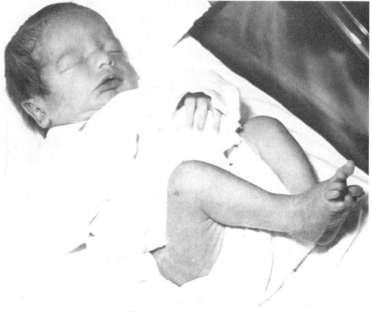

Eric – three days old.

tiny he is. He slept through it all. It'd be kind of nice once in a
while to be allowed to sleep through church like that, wouldn't
it? Especially during some sermons I've heard.

Steve found his first caterpillar of the season last week. Such
a pretty little white one too. Do you remember George of last
year? He rested on the table during each meal one week. He had
a bad ending though — was smashed into our carpet. Sad for the
carpet too.

My beat-up red two-piece sun suit was my sunbathing garb
until a few days ago. I switched to my bathing suit last week. As
I started to lie down on my blanket, Mike rushed up.

"Mommy, do you got a new sun suit?"

I explained it was my bathing suit and definitely wasn't new.

"Just a minute," he said, and rushed off, yelling, "Marsha!
Marta! MARKIE! COME HERE."

A couple of minutes later they all came running, and Mike
was saying, "See . . . See . . . there she is."

They formed a circle around me, were silent for a few sec-
onds, then Marta broke the spell. "Are you wearing your swimming suit?" Then they all giggled. But I stuck it out.

Albert is Libby's new pet. (Libby, who lives two doors away,
will be in second grade this fall.) Albert is a turtle that lives on
bread crumbs, bugs, and raspberries. While Esther and I were sitting in the yard, Libby brought him over to meet us. Esther can't
stand crawling things, so Libby had a fine time exercising Albert
on Esther's driveway. Usually Albert and Libby are good friends,
but one day he lost his temper and bit her on the cheek. (Don't
ask me how a turtle could bite her on the cheek – ask Libby.)
"He might be poison," she said. "If he is, then I'm full of poison,
and I may die." Then she picked up Albert and went home.

Steve and Pat have been going out in the driveway and into
the ditch occasionally, against our strictest rule. Steve is partly
responsible, for sometimes, ever so innocently, he leads Pat
out there.

Bob caught him doing just that the other evening. Steve was
pulling the wagon while Pat pushed it. Running as fast as he
could into Phillips' driveway, Steve was weaving in and out so
Pat would be sure to be dragged through *all* the mud puddles (so

This time, Pat pushes Steve.

good for white shoes too).

Bob dashed out, spanked them both and brought them in the house. Both were broken-hearted, but suddenly Steve stopped crying just long enough to say, "You've got a pretty dress on, Mommy," then broke into tears again.

Love, Jeanne

July 12, 1957

Dear Dad,

Mike has the most wicked looking cut we've seen in some time. While we were gone Saturday night, Richie was pulling him and Steve in our wagon. The wagon tipped over, dumping both boys into the ditch. Neither Mike nor the babysitter know what hit him, but Mike has a big gash close to his left eye, practically in it. Apparently it doesn't bother him much.

Usually Steve has plenty of injuries — skinned nose, scraped shin, scratched arm . . . but recently Mike's had more than his share of wounds. So Steve now has a "sore leg" which we hear about each time Mike is hurt or mentions his injury. Two or three times each night after Steve has gone to bed he comes out to tell us about his sore leg. Invariably Mike has just been up to ask for more antiseptic or a Band-Aid.

Maybe six children will be too many after all. I couldn't teach that many to tie shoestrings! Only six weeks left for Mike to learn so he'll be self-sufficient in kindergarten, so we're making a valiant effort this week. Most complicated thing I've ever tried to do.

This 100° weather is rough for Eric and Pat. Eric has a simple heat rash, but Pat is broken out badly. I made an appointment with the doctor to look at it tomorrow when Eric and I go for our six-week check-up.

Jean Roseberry and Esther came over this afternoon. When I mentioned Pat's terrific heat rash, they looked at each other, both hesitated, then Jean blurted out, "That's not heat rash – that's measles!" Which was especially interesting since we spent yesterday morning with Carol Hamlin and her three children, aged

4, 3, and 1. Her baby is due any day now, and she'd love having everyone catch measles. They WERE our best friends.

No thunder — but plenty of blood around here. Sunday noon I took a sunbath while Bob mowed the lawn. I heard Pat crying so rushed around to the front of the house. I discovered Steve had dumped her out of the wagon (didn't realize that was such a lethal toy). As I picked her up and carried her around to the back, I asked her if she'd like to join Mike down at Marta's swings. She stopped crying and trotted off, and I lay down again on my blanket.

Two minutes later Mike came running up screaming, "Mommy, Mommy, Pat's all bloody — ***all over her.***" As I dashed off, I noticed for the first time the shoulder of my blouse was covered with blood. When Pat saw me coming, she started bellowing again, which brought several neighbors rushing out. Sure enough, blood was gushing down the side of her face and onto her pink and white sun suit (new one, naturally).

Bob ran over, and we took her home and cleaned her up. Under all the blood was just a tiny puncture up under her hair. Of course puncture wounds can be dangerous if they don't bleed properly, but hers had bled enough to clean it out thoroughly. It apparently didn't hurt her as much as might a simple scratch on her knee.

Mike's learning to help me. He makes his own bed every morning, makes his toast and butters it, often cleans off the basement stairs for me.

Saturday Bob offered to take him to the barbershop. Mike said he'd like to go, but ran off and Bob couldn't find him. Feeling sure Mike knew his dad was leaving and just didn't bother to stick around (a favorite trick of his when we say we're going for a ride), Bob went on without him. Nearly 30 minutes later Mike came in sobbing because Daddy had left him.

After he quit crying, he wanted to help me, so I gave him a suit of Eric's to hand-wash. He stood on a chair at the sink and I fixed him lots of soapy water. He had a great time, and the suit had the best sudsing ever.

Imagine leisurely packing a picnic lunch and getting all ready to leave with the four children for a morning in Hamlin's back yard. Esther had come over to borrow our vacuum cleaner and was watching me getting ready to leave. Suddenly I smelled something, glanced out the window, and there, just two houses away, was the big truck oiling the street. Which meant we had about two minutes to get out, or we'd be spending the day at home.

I shouted at Mike and Steve, who were up the street drinking Kool-Aid in a neighbor's yard. Esther grabbed Eric, tossed him in his basket, and rushed him out to the car. Pat and I loaded the diapers, picnic basket, bathing suits (Hamlins have a 4' x 6' pool which was one reason we were going over), and we got out just ahead of the oil truck.

Because of the new oil on the street, I parked the car a block away when we came home. Mike had a swimming lesson scheduled, which meant Steve, Pat, Eric and I would normally go to the wading pool. But it was so hot (95^0) that I asked Susan (neighbor) to stay with the younger three, and I went swimming with Mike. He's almost learned to float on his back and stomach.

During his lesson I was at the far end of the pool trying to swim. (I've forgotten about everything I learned two years ago when I took Adult Education lessons.) A man there with his son took pity on me and showed me how to breathe properly – rather, had his son show me. He thought he'd seen me at Junior High PTA meeting which was a great blow to my pride, since my oldest child isn't even in school. We all have to grow old someday – but let's use the word "mature."

Love, Jeanne

P.S. MIKE CAN TIE HIS SHOE STRINGS!!!

J

July 17, 1957

Dear Dad,

Eric and I went back to the doctor for our six-week checkup Saturday, and the doctor said Eric hasn't been getting enough to eat. He weighed 8 pounds 9 ounces, after 6 pounds 4 ounces at birth. So now I'm spooning all kinds of solid food into him and we're getting along much better.

Before yesterday, he'd been fine as long as I nursed him every three or four hours, including nights, which I didn't like at all.

This week he's doing better, sleeping nights, mostly. I do have to give him an occasional bottle, which he doesn't appreciate, but guess I'd better.

It's harder to get enough sleep lately, mainly because we don't put the boys to bed until 8 or 8:30, and I don't want to go to bed before they do. Solar is on their own daylight savings schedule which means we get up at 5:30 in order for Bob to leave by 6:20. Always before, the children have gotten up with us, but now I insist they stay in bed until 7 a.m. It's nice to have 1 1/2 hours quiet before bedlam breaks loose.

Mike is our most difficult — but isn't the oldest always? Pat is spoiled too, which was the big reason we'd have liked another girl this time. With three brothers, I wonder . . . but she's crazy about Eric. She throws a tantrum whenever Steve or Mike sits on my lap, but thinks it's fine for me to hold Eric.

Today is another 100° day and I'm sitting out in the back yard with the card table and lawn chair writing this. The children are playing in the sprinkler, a neighbor has theirs on too, so all the children have a gay time running back and forth.

We seem to gravitate toward friends with big families. Our

block has two other families with four, while our two closest
friends have four each — in fact, one, Carol Hamlin, just had her
fourth Monday. Max and their other three children are coming
here for supper tonight. (Hamburgers because they're easy, and
because it's the only thing that all six children will eat.)

Ecklunds (Bob E. was best man at our wedding and works at
Solar now) have four boys, one 5, twins will be 3 in October, and
David 1 in October. They're expecting another next March. They
don't plan to have any more. In fact, I think he's going to be ster-
ilized. They'd been planning to before she got pregnant this time
— what a surprise that was!

I'd hate to have either of us operated on, but I do hope I don't
get pregnant for about two years — if then. If we do decide to go
on and have two more as we've always planned, I hope we can
stop then.

This morning a friend helped me cut Pat's hair for the first
time. She's had braids (little ones), which looked cute for about
five minutes after being combed. Then last week she developed

Pat with her hair cut. The brother pushing her seems to have a gun???

Even Eric likes to watch the planes take off.

that horrible heat rash – the neighbors were positive it was measles – so we took her to the doctor and he said it definitely was a rash.

It's much better this week, but cutting her hair seemed necessary for her scalp was broken out. It worries us for last year her heat rash got infected and she had to take penicillin. We hope to avoid that this year. Her short hair looks as cute, better actually, when I remember that I couldn't keep it combed the other way.

Do you remember Peg Wood from college? She invited us to visit her and her family (four daughters). However, we've resolved never to visit friends overnight with all our children, for we think it'd probably be the quickest way to lose friends. It'd be so much fun to see her though. Maybe we'll visit them some day.

I dieted like crazy the last three months of pregnancy because I'd gained 18 pounds at six months, and I avoided gaining any more. However, I only lost 14 of the 18, which is depressing. I haven't managed to diet since I got home despite all my resolutions.

Last Sunday afternoon we all went out to the airport to watch the planes. Even Eric got excited when a plane took off. We go out there fairly often because the children all enjoy it.

Love, Jeanne

August 14, 1957

Dear Dad,

Ten days ago we celebrated Mike's fifth birthday. No longer do we have four under five!

It's been extremely luxurious to have Eric two months old. I wasn't as philosophical as I should have been about getting up nights with him. But now he's an absolute angel about sleeping through the night. He's been so much easier to care for almost exactly since his second birthday (monthly birthday, that is).

Steve, Marcia Derby, Mike – Happy birthday, Mike!

Remind me of this next time I'm fussing about the trouble involved with the care of a new baby.

Last night Eric was in bed by 7:15, and we didn't hear a word out of him until after 6:30 this morning — after Bob and I had finished our breakfast. And even then he wasn't desperately hungry — just seemed glad to see us. He smiles so cute now — and Bob is infuriating when he says, "It's just gas!"

Last night's rain was beautiful. I'm writing this outside on our card table so that if the children get too too muddy, I can stop them as they run in the house (except there's no one to guard the front door). The thunderstorm started about 6:30 last night, and we got a bit exasperated with Steve — Pat, too.

Bob and I love to watch a storm coming up, and enjoy the thunder and lightning. But about half our neighbors are afraid of storms. Esther, next door, always takes her entire family down to the basement, especially if it happens in the middle of the night. Therefore, Steve thinks it's the proper thing to do to say he's afraid and act as if he is.

He probably is by now, after all the pretending he's done. So last night he had Pat screaming along with him. Believe me, we're nice to them, within reason, but we do think it's partly imagination.

Two weeks from today Mike will start school. The new building across the field behind our house won't be finished for two or three months. During that time they'll hold split sessions in the two houses they've been using for schoolhouses for the past two or three years. Since Mike will probably go to kindergarten afternoon session, it won't shorten his time at school.

A couple of weeks ago we all walked over to see Mike's school. It was Eric's first trip in the wagon and he loved it. When Pat was little, Steve used to pull her, and Mike did the same when Steve was a baby.

I'd assumed I'd have help with Eric from Pat, but no. She's smart (or lazy). She hopped right in beside Eric, lay flat on her stomach in the identical position he was in, and rode the entire way. It was a trifle crowded, but Eric didn't mind in the least. Since then we've taken several "walks" in this way.

After seeing these school buildings, I got a much clearer

picture of the desperate need for new schools. Some classes will be held in the basement. It (the basement) wasn't even painted, had inadequate lighting, and cement floor just like our basement . . . not at all attractive. The new building will be very nice, however.

With Steve pushing, both Pat and Eric get a ride.

Dorothy Thompson has an interesting article in the current *Ladies Home Journal*. She's all for building schools, but thinks many buildings being constructed are much too extravagant.

Pat's having a rough time with her mouth. More than a week ago she was on Steve's trike in our front yard. Carla (who is her age and certainly couldn't be blamed for the accident) pushed the trike down the incline, and Pat fell onto the cement driveway.

This happened about 5 p.m., and Pat cried most of the evening until we put her to bed. She couldn't eat a thing that evening, for besides being chipped some more, her top front teeth were loosened. By next morning, however, she could eat although she still couldn't handle hard things like bread crusts. (Of course I didn't fix toast for her.)

Her cheek was quite swollen for several days, but she seemed to be all right — until we had roasting ears. She tried to eat one, then started to cry. She managed the corn all right, though, when I cut it off the ear for her.

Then two days ago she slipped on our front step and loosened the teeth again. Her gums look awful, and her mouth bled a lot again. However, she hasn't had much trouble eating this time. She's learned to chew with her side teeth — it's interesting to see her gnaw at a cookie.

We called our dentist. He said that unless she was in terrible pain (which she isn't so long as she doesn't fall again), there's nothing he can do and it's nothing to worry about. The teeth tighten up automatically, I guess. She's a sweet little thing and rather enjoys opening her mouth and showing us (and the neighbors) when asked — and manages to put on such a pathetic, woebegone expression, it's almost funny.

The night Pat first fell and cried all evening was a confusing one. About 3:30 that afternoon Bob and Jerry Johnson called and said they were in town with their two children. They're friends from Wichita, and we hadn't seen them for 11/2 years. Of course I invited them to supper.

I couldn't get Bob on the phone until nearly 5 p.m. to ask him to bring chicken home for supper. Pat got hurt at 5:00. At 5:30 Pat was still crying (I was holding her in the front yard), Eric was crying for supper (I couldn't possibly leave Pat to feed him), Bob wasn't home yet with the groceries, even if I'd had time to start supper, and at that point our guests drove in! Of course we eventually had supper. When Bob arrived about 6 p.m., Bob Johnson commented that he bet I'd never been so glad to see my husband in my life!

The main thing that bothered me was that we'll probably not see the Johnsons again for another year or two, and I don't want them to think we live like that all the time. I like to pretend, at least, that with four children under 5, we can still lead a calm and peaceful life. And much of the time I believe it.

The other day Marcia came down to play house with Mike and Steve. Steve was to be Daddy, so he went over to the wagon and flopped down for a rest. Marcia said, "Oh Steve, don't do that. Daddies don't rest."

"Mine does!" answered Steve, and refused to budge.

When I told Barbara (Marcia's mother) about it she surprised me by getting serious, sighing, and saying she guessed the children didn't see their father rest much. I had the impression that she wouldn't ask him to help with the dishes that night.

Love, Jeanne

August 26, 1957

Dear Dad,

Pat's front teeth still seem to be loose — Bob is almost sure they'll come out. I took her to the dentist a week ago, and much to my surprise, she played shy (and I'd been so proud that she's friendly and not afraid of anyone). She refused to open her mouth for him, but he's positive there's nothing to worry about. He said they'd tighten up again, and he probably knows.

Mike had his teeth cleaned for the first time that day, and behaved beautifully. Steve was angelic about letting the dental technician "count" his teeth. Eric stayed with Esther next door, and I paid Janice to go with me to look after Pat and keep an eye on Mike and Steve while my teeth were being cleaned.

The most difficult and most tiring job of being mother of three or four small children is taking them to the doctor, dentist, or, perhaps even worse, shopping. I've taken them to downtown Des Moines only once by myself since Pat was born, and then only to one store. I certainly haven't tried it with Eric. Of course we do most of our shopping in West Des Moines anyhow.

Every day or two a salesman comes to our door selling something "for the good of our children." Invariably he starts with the question, "Are you interested in your children's education?"

Bob and I have had the urge several times to say, "No. That's the school's job," just to see the salesman's shocked expression. Until the other day we'd resisted the impulse. But this man came while all four children were clamoring for lunch.

To top it off, the salesman was hard of hearing, and came into the house a trifle rudely. He was selling *Child World*. (I still don't know what that is, and care less.) I told him I didn't have time, even a minute, to talk with him.

I pride myself on being courteous with salesmen, even as I send them away promptly, but this one either was too deaf to hear me or pretended he was. Anyhow, as he went on his way, he was shouting back at me, "You mean you have four children and you don't care about their education?"

"That's right!" I cheerfully responded.

Mike and Steve washed their trikes yesterday. They submitted to scrubbing them off with the sponge and soapy water only because Bob told them they could rinse with the hose. While they were spraying, they looked positively ecstatic.

Steve is proud of his clean trike.

Mike carefully scrubs his tricycle.

Saturday night we had supper with Hamlins. On the way over we solemnly talked to Mike and Steve about manners . . . don't talk about food you don't like, eat a little of everything, etc. They listened intently . . . then ate their ham and potatoes and carefully avoided the lima beans and salad as usual. Guess they figured if it wasn't nice to talk about the food, we shouldn't talk about it to the point of insisting they taste things. Which makes sense, I have to admit.

Eric has been on a three meals a day schedule now for almost a full week (with one or two exceptions) and it's wonderful. He still sleeps most of the time. Several afternoons he's awakened about 4:00, which means we can take him (and Pat) for a ride in the wagon.

The "Getting Your Child Ready for Kindergarten" booklet says a child should have the opportunity to feed and care for either a pet or a smaller brother or sister. So Mike is helping me dress Pat now.

Yesterday morning while I was feeding Eric, Mike tied Steve's shoestrings, and completely dressed Pat. He put her panties and dress on her . . . even tied her sash, and did a pretty good job. Then he laid her on her back, and had her put her feet straight up in the air while he put her socks and shoes on her. Her shoes are hard to put on, so he stuck her toes in them, then pounded on the soles (with her feet still up in the air) until they slid on. Pat loved it. Then he combed her hair. I wish she'd stand that still for me.

Mike is exasperated with me because I haven't ordered his red boots for school yet. I plan to phone Sears about them today. He wanted me to call them at 7:00 this morning. Did I tell you we bought him a yellow Roy Rogers raincoat for his birthday? He's thrilled every day it rains or even sprinkles, for it means he can go outside wearing his raincoat.

Love, Jeanne

August 29, 1957

Mike's first day at school was a rainy one.

Dear Dad,

Today is our first day of school. Mike is to be there by 1 p.m. with his name, address, and phone number in his mind, $1.50 in his pocket, and the ability to tie his shoes. Everything but the phone number is well under control and we're working on that. I've never been able to remember phone numbers, and he seems to have the same trouble.

I've asked Pam (from next door) to stay with Steve, Pat, and Eric while I walk to school with Mike . . . but when I asked Mike if he'd like me to go with him, he informed me mommies aren't supposed to go. Bob suggested that if Mike doesn't think I should go at the last minute, I take the camera and tell him I want his picture as he goes into the building.

I do want to go, although I'm proud of his independence. He's been walking over every day or two the past couple of weeks, partly to see how the new building is progressing.

Did I tell you about his first trip over alone? It was a rainy morning, his first chance to wear his new raincoat. I suggested he might walk over to his schoolhouse by himself. At first he wasn't sure he understood me, but then he was eager. It was an odd feeling to see him walking so far down the street all alone, and then disappearing around the corner.

While Mike was gone, Steve and Pat helped me start some cookies so we could have a party when Mike returned. I sometimes think Steve is more thrilled than Mike about school.

Barbara (whose Carla is eight days younger than Pat, and Mary Beth two days younger than Eric) had Carla and Mary Beth in their wagon yesterday afternoon. Steve was pulling ours, and had gone up our driveway. I asked him to let me turn it around, telling him that's when it's apt to tip over. I added that Mike tipped him out once when he was a baby.

Barbara was a few feet away, listening, then absent-mindedly turned hers around — and dumped both girls out! Luckily they fell on the grass. Both (or should I include Barbara and say three?) were frightened but not hurt.

The rainy days this week have been fun, although noisy. Tuesday I sorted through my recipe cards, discarding a lot of them that I knew I'd never use. Since I have stacks of recipes to paste, which will take many cards, I decided, silly as it may sound, to reuse the cards. So I had all three children sit around the kitchen table, gave them each a stack of recipe cards, and had them tear off the old recipes. Even Pat helped quite a bit. Janice and Pam came to the door for some reason, and I invited them in. Thanks to all of them, all my cards are now ready to be reused. (Should I check into the child labor laws?)

Also Tuesday the boys were coloring, cutting, and pasting. I only had one bottle of glue, so after watching and hearing them fight over it for a while, I set the timer in front of them, and gave each boy two minutes for his turn. Then they each had a wonderful time trying their best to use all the glue before it went to the other one.

That night Bob suggested I make flour and water paste, which I hadn't thought of. So yesterday each one (including Pat — what a mess!) had his/her own measuring cup of paste. They didn't have half as much fun with nothing to fight about.

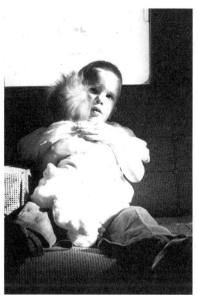 

Serious Mike, goofy Steve hold Pat. (1956)

One incident has convinced me that Mike and Steve have quite different personalities. Up until now, we'd usually brushed off any differences as being due mostly to 19 months difference in age. But to get to the point — in our photograph album is a page of pictures of Mike, at Steve's present age (3 1/2), holding Pat, very carefully and nicely. On the opposite page is Steve, 2 . . . she's on his lap, but she's staying there mostly through the force of gravity, not because of his care.

Mike has held Eric occasionally for me, very nicely, of course, which I thought was because of his age. But when I give Eric to Steve, Steve (now 3 1/2) still looks all around, giggles, and has a whee of a time, but doesn't bother to hang on to Eric. (We love all three boys — a lot! Pat too!)

Love, Jeanne

P.S. Mike let us walk with him to school, but when I started to go up the steps with him, he stopped me.

"You can go home now," he said.

J

October 7, 1957

Dear Dad,

Big news! Mike was a brownie. You see, the quietest child during rest period in kindergarten is allowed to use the brownie or fairy stick to awaken the other children. I had begun to wonder if Mike would ever be quiet enough. But the other day he came home announcing he'd been the brownie.

I was thrilled and asked if he'd been that quiet. "No, I didn't have my eyes shut — but I turned my head the other way and Mrs. Amick couldn't see."

Pat is now two. Yesterday for her birthday I suggested that Mike and Steve each make her a birthday card. So they each drew and colored a picture for her, then watched me write "Happy Birthday to Pat from Mike/Steve" on them. She was so pleased.

Her birthday party was today. Because she likes the women better than the children (the grownups spoil her), I invited the mothers, too. So we had nine noise-making children, two babies, and six mothers. It was awfully confusing, and next year I plan only to invite the three little girls who are about Pat's age.

She wore her new red dress, and sat on Esther's lap for half the morning, holding her new Elsie doll. Of course she had fun blowing out her two candles, eating her cake, and licking the drips on her ice cream cone.

The Solar Flying Club gave free plane rides to Solar families yesterday. We went out right after church, but even then we were numbers 290-295, and they were giving rides at that time to number 30 or 40. About 1:30 Bob suggested that Pat, Eric, and I come on home, which we did. We all took a nap, then went back

Pat enjoyed her second birthday ice cream cone.

out about 5 p.m.

Mike was just getting off the plane — it still wasn't his turn, but a man had let him go in his place. After all that waiting, it looked as if Steve wouldn't get to go for they were just to number 260 for the last ride — but a man told Steve and Bob to go ahead. I could have hugged that man (but didn't because his wife was right beside him). Steve was practically flying himself when he got off, he was so thrilled. Today he's still talking about the trees, cars, and river he saw.

Saturday Bob went down to work as usual. About 10:30 he phoned to say he was tired of work and wanted to take us over to Boone for a picnic at the Ledges. I don't remember being there before, although he says we were when we lived in Ames. We had a wonderful time.

All the children slept on the trip over, and Bob and I enjoyed the trees so much. It was a beautiful day. Several bees joined us for lunch which made me nervous, but none of us were stung. Then we took a short walk, but decided our children aren't quite ready to climb steep bluffs yet.

I forgot to tell you – last month when we visited Bob's par-

ents, Bob and his dad took Steve and Mike fishing. First, Grandpa dug up the worms, then they all tried their hand. I wish they could go fishing with you, Dad.

Love,
Jeanne

Steve: "This fishing takes patience!"

Mike helps Daddy fish.

Special insert in 10/7 letter

The Hamlin Invasion

It's almost a week now since the Hamlins went home. Life is practically back to normal. And Eric is eating again.

At approximately 9 a.m. Friday, September 27, Marcie (almost 4), David (almost 2), and Jeanne (2½ months) came in — with Max and Carol and a box of pajamas, jeans, shirts, socks, and a dozen diapers (in case I ran out). At 9:30 Max and Carol left. Mark (almost 5) didn't come until Monday morning because he was visiting his grandparents.

Life was remarkably peaceful for at least an hour. Mike was outdoors and didn't know they'd come until noon. Marcie and Steve went down to the basement to play. All was quiet . . . until I heard Steve say, "But you won't let me play with your toys at your house — so you can't have mine either!" And so it went, for four days.

Marcie and I had a fine time Friday afternoon and Saturday. When I wouldn't let her take a toy away from David, or hit somebody, she'd either scream, bite herself (never anyone else), pull her own hair, or chant over and over, "I don't want to go to Lindsay's. I don't want to go to Lindsay's . . ." Occasionally she threatened to take off her shoes. I suggested her feet might get a bit chilly. She looked a trifle surprised, and left them on that time.

By Sunday both Marcie and David were calling me "Mommie" all the time. (I don't know why for they both certainly know my name.) When Carol came after them Tuesday, Marcie told her she didn't want to go home. And today Carol told me

she offered to let Marcie have a birthday party in November and
invite whomever she wanted. She said she wanted Lindsays . . .
so I guess we got along all right.

Pat had worried me a little before they came. She and Carla
(neighbor who is one week younger) don't get along at all
— constantly hit and push each other. David is a month younger,
and I could just imagine living with that for four days. But they
got along beautifully. David is a little darling anyhow. While
he was here, I certainly didn't need a puppy for he followed me
around just like one. He and Pat would sit on the sectional for an
hour together just looking at books . . . and not fight at all!

Although Jeanne is six weeks younger than Eric, she's bigger.
We think they look entirely different. But almost every time I
held Jeanne, either Mike or Steve would ask if it was Eric, and
vice-versa. Not only do they not look alike — they acted entirely
different. And I'm grateful Jeanne didn't follow Eric's example.
About Sunday he decided not to eat. All day Monday and Tuesday morning he ate very little — and wasn't at all happy. Every
night they were here he woke up for a night feeding, and he
hadn't done that for two months. But two hours after they went
home, he started eating again. He's fine now. I hope it doesn't
mean he's the nervous type. He should be used to confusion.

Saturday afternoon we went downtown after a package at
Sear's. One store was having an open house with free coffee,

Eric – four months old

doughnuts, and balloons for the kiddies. I wanted us to go in, Bob and I, with our seven children, but we didn't quite have the nerve. Sunday afternoon we went out to a farm after apples. A couple of girls came over to the car and asked if the babies were twins. I felt sorry about disillusioning them.

Max accused Bob last week of teaching his children bad habits. David has always loved going to bed, and behaved beautifully at bedtime here. But his first night home, he refused to go to bed. By bad habits, I wonder if he could also have been referring to cereal. None of our children will put milk on dry cereal. The first two mornings Marcie asked for milk, but by Monday she decided she couldn't eat it that way either. I wonder what else she copied.

Four children in diapers was interesting — but I'm glad I don't live with them all. One morning I had three dirty diapers in five minutes — Pat didn't perform that time.

We've always liked hamburgers, but I'm not sure we'll have them again soon. That's almost the only thing all the Hamlin and Lindsay kids will eat, so we had them Friday, Saturday, and Monday nights. Sunday we had ham. For lunch we had peanut butter and jelly sandwiches twice and a choice of tuna or cheese twice. Each morning about 9:30 when there was a lull, I'd make all the sandwiches and refrigerate them. Then all I had to do at noon was toss one on each plate, cut up apples, or serve Jello.

It was rather hectic — and I don't think I was ever so tired in my life as I was Saturday night — but, amazing as it seems, I was almost sorry to see them go Tuesday. They all kissed me goodbye so sweetly.

Max and Carol said they had a wonderful time — played tennis every day, read, went for a walk in the woods, etc.

Love, Jeanne

*Bob was gone
Thursday and
Friday nights,
so we all got up
Saturday morning
at 5:30 a.m. so he
could be involved.*

*We make the Jack
'o lanterns together.
Mike's is cleaned out
beautifully, and Pat is
working hard at
getting hers done.*

*We'll soon be ready
to greet the trick or
treaters with three
grinning jack 'o
lanterns.*

November 7, 1957

Dear Dad,

We had the most wonderful time Halloween.

It was Pat's first night playing Trick or Treat. Mike wore his frog costume, Steve his tiger one, both left from last year. I put a dark dress of mine on Pat, pinning it up so it was almost floor length on her. Then, for a cape, I draped a dark piece of material around her shoulders. I'd planned to make a pointed witch's cap but forgot to buy construction paper for it, so dug up an old black velvet hat of mine. It had a plume and a veil over her face and was quite satisfactory. She carried a little broom every step of the way.

At the first two houses she sang the first two lines of "Rock a Bye Baby," but decided it wasn't necessary after that. At Philips' and Cervetti's (both next door neighbors) she went in with the boys, but didn't come out with them. I waited and waited, and finally went in after her. There she was, in the living room at each house. She'd taken off her hat, was sitting on the floor eating her candy and visiting with the neighbors. It took some tall talking to get her out happily.

Yesterday was my first conference with Mike's teacher. (We have three or four conferences each year instead of report cards here.) She showed me pictures he had drawn at the first of the year and the one he made yesterday, in order to illustrate how he had improved. She mentioned that he sings at least as well as the average child of his age. This was a relief to me for I was afraid he might have inherited my inability to carry a tune.

Lyle Schwilling, a friend of mine in college who worked at the *Tribune News* in Manhattan when I did, stopped to see us one Sunday evening recently. His wife, whom we'd never met, was with him. They've been married about three years and live in Kansas City. The next day Mike and Steve wanted to know if they had any children.

When I said no, Mike said, "Why? Couldn't they buy any?"

"I know," Steve said, "maybe they could have some of us."

"No, they couldn't," answered Mike. "We're Lindsays."

When can you visit us? We finally had Eric baptized last Sunday. He's so cute now. I wish you could see him. Could you spend Christmas with us in Arthur? Mother and Dad Lindsay were here Sunday, and Mother said something about your coming. She'd like to have you, and of course we would. We'll probably drive to Arthur Monday evening, and come home Christmas afternoon (Wednesday).

All of us but Eric had the flu but are fine now. The worst day was Bob's second day home, when he, Mike, and Steve were all sick but not sick enough to be in bed. I threatened to leave either the boys or Bob with Nadean, my neighbor. She said she'd choose Mike and Steve, judging from the way her husband acts when he's sick. Seriously, Bob is very considerate even when he's sick, but the feuding and fussing between the boys, which is bad enough any time, and much worse when they're ill, naturally bothered him.

I've been attempting to straighten our basement a little. We don't dare move away from here because we couldn't face taking everything out of our basement.

Solar had another shake-up last week, and our two best friends were laid off, Max Hamlin and Bob Ecklund. Ecklunds would like to stay in Des Moines if Bob E. can find a job. They're rather sad about the situation. Max and Carol, however, had been half wanting to leave for some time, and don't seem bothered much. They might even find a job here and stay, too. Because of the reorganization, Bob has 63 people working for him now instead of the 20 he started with a month ago. He feels fairly secure.

The other night Mike, Steve, and Eric were all in bed before Pat had had her bath which is unusual, for she usually goes to bed first. So we (Pat and I) decided to have a bubble bath. We

had a wonderful time. I shaved my legs, so she took my com-
plexion brush, lifted her leg above the suds, and "shaved" for
all she was worth. Then we both washed our hair, and rinsed it
under the shower. The most luxurious part of it for me was that,
after I showed her how, she did a lovely job of scrubbing my
back with the brush. Bob laughed and laughed when he saw her
and told her she was being rooked, but she didn't seem to mind.

Later Pat didn't want to go to bed, and I didn't want to make
her cry. So we told her that bear and Elsie (Her Borden cow doll)
were so tired, and she'd better take them to bed. (We used to do
that with Mike and Steve, and they'd immediately trot off to bed
with their toys, as docilely as you please.)

Pat looked very serious, picked them up, said, "Poor bear.
Poor Elsie. Tired." Then she trotted off to the bedroom with
them. I followed her, planning to tuck her in. But she fooled me
— she tucked them in, then darted back out into the living room.
After all, it was her kids, not her, who were tired!

Mike helped me clean house this morning. He vacuumed the
living room. He also cleans the bathroom for me quite often. I
think I'll let him make a batch of gingerbread from a mix pretty
soon. I'll see if he's old enough to use the electric mixer.

I told you, didn't I, that we can't possibly drive to Kansas for
Thanksgiving? I have no idea where Betty got that idea.

Your hogs must have done well. You're going to keep the
feeder hogs through the winter, are you?

Do you see much of Cleora now? We're always happy to hear
about her. It would be so nice if you two could be married. If
I've mentioned this before, please forgive me for repeating it, for
I guess it really isn't my business, is it? But I don't like to think
of you living alone.

Love, Jeanne

PART II

1958
No More Babies!

Steve, Pat, and Mike make Christmas cookies with Eric's help.

January 16, 1958

Dear Dad,

I'm enclosing a picture of our Christmas cookie making. As you can see, Eric was right in the middle of it.

We're having our first bout with childhood diseases — chicken pox. Mike got it first. We received the little note right before Christmas saying "Your son has been exposed to chickenpox . . . " He didn't break out until Dec. 30, bless his heart, for by then all our Christmas activities were over, except for New Year's Eve. Luckily the sitter had had chicken pox.

Then promptly last weekend, Steve, Pat and Eric broke out. The boys were scarcely sick at all. I'm glad Pat was the last to get it, for she's rather miserable. If all four had been this sick, it would have been hard for all of us.

There may be a bright spot, though — Pat's not toilet trained at all. I haven't gotten excited about it, figuring that eventually she'd more or less train herself. But a couple of days ago she was so broken out across her tummy that I put panties on her so she'd be more comfortable. Bless me, if she hasn't started going to the toilet at least part of the time.

I realize, of course, that Pat'll probably be back in diapers when the novelty wears off, but I can't help hoping. After all, she was two last October. She expresses herself as well as Mike and Steve did at 3, I think. It seems slightly ridiculous for her to discuss this diaper situation at great lengths with me, yet she refuses to use the toilet. She tells me she's still a baby (largely because the boys play house so much and she's always their baby), and *should* wear diapers.

Mike has been going to afternoon kindergarten but next week

switches to morning. Since he's been gone only while the rest of us nap, this will actually be the first time school has made much difference around here. He and Steve fuss a lot, so I think it will be more peaceful with just Steve and Pat to tease each other in the mornings.

Eric loves to be out on the floor with them, and I think I'd just put the playpen away if it weren't for one floor lamp we have. He dives for the cord the minute he's out, and yesterday pulled it over on his head, which of course was quite a shock. (Luckily, not an electric shock.)

Thank goodness Steve and Pat are well enough to play in the snow this morning. We gave them a snow disk for Christmas, and they're having a great time.

Pat – Trudging up hill is hard, so hard I have to rest a minute.

Eric is still little — about 15 pounds now. He has a couple of teeth and very recently started crawling (not very speedy yet). He's a lot of fun now. Carol Hamlin, a close friend of mine who has four children about the ages of ours, just discovered she's going to have another baby next August, and isn't very thrilled about it. (She's Catholic, so at least has an excuse.)

As I told her, I look at Eric and can't feel too sorry for her for having one like him around again a year from now. (She's the type who definitely doesn't want sympathy even though she'd have rather waited two or three years before having another one.) I still don't especially want to follow her example though! Especially since they're moving to Los Angeles next month.

Steve pilots with Pat as passenger.

We hate to see them go. We exchanged dinners quite a bit, usually including all the children, and last fall, as you may remember, I kept her four for four days. They were to keep ours this spring as soon as I weaned Eric so Bob and I could go on a vacation over a long weekend. But because they knew they'd be moving, they kept ours the weekend of Dec. 13. Bob and I had a wonderful time not doing much of anything, and pretending Eric was our only child. It was a great way to celebrate my birthday!

Steve and Mike got red slippers for Christmas. Quite often Steve wakes up before I do in the afternoon, and recently he's started playing fairly quietly for 30 minutes or so until I get up. But he invariably comes in to have me tie his shoes. But the day after Christmas he got up, came in and said, "See, Mommy, I put on my slippers so I wouldn't have to wake you to tie my shoes!"

He's a character, either as funny as he can be, or perfectly awful. He can think of more excuses to get out of bed at night than the rest of them put together. He nearly always wears either Bob's white navy cap or his old Boy Scout cap, saying that's his army hat.

Love, Jeanne

March 3, 1958

Dear Dad,

Steve's fourth birthday party was today. Since his birthday was Saturday, I'd planned to have the party Friday, but Mark Howell had chicken pox last week. We postponed it so he could come. But this morning Marcie Derby had croup — we can't win! Mark, Carla Derby (Pat's age) and Tommy (3 1/2) and Kathi (5) Waters came at 10 a.m. to play. Tommy and Kathi are not neighbors, but we invited them because we had room for eight around the table, and mainly because we like them.

At noon Marta Howell came home from kindergarten with Mike for lunch. We had hamburgers, of course, with potato chips, carrot sticks, ice cream cones and birthday cake (angel food with chocolate frosting). The children all behaved remarkably well.

Steve liked your birthday card. It came promptly on Saturday and he opened it at noon at the table. We had his family birthday dinner at that time because Bob and I had company that evening.

We got Steve a Playskool tractor, one with a wrench and screwdriver, and he can take it all apart. He likes it a lot. We also bought a small roll of scotch tape, box of colors, and cheap typing paper for each boy. We put them in a box along with a pencil, eraser, and scissors. They call it their "desk." Mike even has a ballpoint pen in his.

We've been giving them an allowance of 3¢ (Steve) and 5¢ (Mike) a week for a couple of months. They each take 1¢ to Sunday School and have been saving the rest. Now they want to get to a store and spend part of their savings for a small jar of paste. Oh yes, we've raised Steve's allowance to 4¢ now that he's 4.

Eric helps Jeanne Hamlin take her bath.

Last month, before they left for California, Carol and three of
their children, Jeanne, Marcia, and David, spent five days with
us. We're going to miss them.

This has been a hectic day for Eric. He's been standing up
at the sectional for some time, and stood up in his playpen for
the first time today. Evidently he can get down quite easily from
these places. But he learned to pull himself up in his crib yesterday and still doesn't know how to get down. So each nap is quite
a production.

I lay him down and cover him up, then shut the door. He
stands up, starts crying because he can't get back down. After a
short time, I go in, lay him down again, and shut the door. Again
he stands up, again he starts screaming. After about three or four
times of going through this, he finally goes to sleep. I remember
going through the same thing with the other children. It usually
takes two or three days to learn the great art of sitting down.

Last week Steve got stuck in the mud behind Derbys' house.
Bill Roseberry pulled him out and Johnny (about 8) brought
Steve home, carrying one boot and wearing the other. The under-
statement of the year was Johnny saying, as I came to the door,
"Steve's a little messed up!" I was surprised that the one shoe
recovered from all the mud – it was absolutely covered inside
and out.

Barbara Derby said she guesses pulling Steve out of the mud
is just part of spring. Last year it was Bob Derby who pulled him
out. He (Steve) really gets mired in to where he can't possibly
move by himself.

We bought a high fidelity record player last week and we're
thrilled. It's a bit delicate — if the children run or jump in the
living room (or even if I walk heavily), the needle jumps.

Today I played "Swan Lake" while the children were eating
lunch. I heard Mike telling the others, "You can't play cowboys
and Indians while the new record player is going because it
spoils it. You have to go down in the basement."

Woody and Audrey Speer came over for dinner Friday night.
He's Bob's assistant at Solar. I met them at the Christmas party
but we'd never had them here before. I followed a menu I found
in a magazine, so practically everything we ate was different
than anything we'd had before.

We had rolled steak with a bacon-rice stuffing. It tasted good,
but the steak split while cooking, so it wasn't pretty — just
sloppy looking. I served it with a current-consommé sauce
(beef consommé and current jelly mixed — tasted better than
it sounds), potatoes mashed with sour cream and cream cheese,
then browned in the oven, "green beans supreme" (dried onion
soup and mushrooms added to cooked beans), tossed salad,
lemon cheese cake, and coffee. I liked everything but Bob wasn't
quite so enthusiastic. I hope our guests did.

This Friday night we're having Jacques and Shirley Foster
over and I'm trying another menu, but I think it's a little simpler.
It's another meat roll — maybe it will stay together.

Bob and Kelly Ecklund asked Bob and me to be godparents
of Doug, their new baby. They were going to have him baptized
yesterday, but several of them had colds so they had to postpone
it. They may do it next Sunday.

They still haven't found a place to live in Keokuk and are
getting eager to move. They seem to have a rough time no matter
what they do. One night last week Kelly called to tell me David
had a temperature of 103, Steve (Ecklund) had come home at 9
a.m. instead of going on into kindergarten because he doesn't
like school, their cat was just home from the vet — the cat

Eric – "Steve, you're so silly!

had ear mites — and Doug was constipated (which seems a little ridiculous for a three-week-old baby). Sometimes Kelly looks kind of hard for trouble.

Were Betty and I much alike when we were little? Steve and Mike certainly aren't. Steve will undoubtedly be the salesman or politician from our family — Mike will try twice as hard, probably with less results, because Steve knows the value of blarney.

A good example of their two personalities — at supper the other day, Steve looked at his fried potatoes, which he loves, and said, "Oh, you're a nice mommy!"

Mike looked up and said, "WHY?"

You should see Pat. Eric wants to play under the table where I'm typing and she doesn't approve. The first time she pulled him out by one foot while he was sitting straight up. (I didn't suppose Eric had enough strength to sit up through that.) Now she's decided an easier method is to pull him out by both feet while he's on his stomach. Eric thinks it's a wonderful game, and goes right back so he'll get another ride, but Pat is getting frustrated.

Bob is disappointed in me. You know I've wanted Eric's hair cut ever since he was born, but Bob hasn't agreed. Last week Merze Seeberger, a friend who hadn't seen Eric since he was a month old, was coming over. I didn't want her to see him with such long hair, so I took the scissors and did a little chopping. It didn't take me long to realize this was no job for me, but in the meantime, I made two or three very unwise swaths. If I'd kept up, he would've made a good looking Mennonite with his bowl cut.

Love, Jeanne

March 10, 1958

Dear Dad,

I just got a letter from Carol Hamlin. As you know, she and Max moved to California a couple of weeks ago. Her letter was fascinating. I hope someday I can travel a little so I won't be so amazed to hear about things slightly different from Iowa and Kansas. For example, she mentioned wading into the ocean – and I've never even seen an ocean.

She also wrote about her neighbors being quite different from each other. Sometimes I think our neighbors are too much alike. We never see anyone over 35 or under 25, except for children under 10. But when we start talking, we find we're not all the same after all.

Bob and Nadean Phillips came over for dinner at 7. Pam was with them, but she went right to bed in our room. Before we bought our hi-fi record player a couple of weeks ago, Bob asked Bob P., who works at Graybar, for hi-fi literature. Bob P. told us about this wonderful bargain which we couldn't resist.

Anyhow, to get back to the subject, a mutual friend lent Bob Phillips his "Music Man" LP record to bring over here to play on our hi-fi. So we spent the evening listening to Meredith Wilson's Iowa songs. I'd heard part of it on the radio, and would love to have the record, but we can't even pay for the hi-fi until we get our income tax refund. So no records for a while!

We've wanted hi-fi for years – much worse than TV, but felt TV was sort of a necessity a year ago. I can remember figuring out where we could put it (a hi-fi) in our little house on 54th. So of course we're both thrilled – although it wasn't the smartest thing we could do financially. We're all right as long as the government comes through with our tax refund by April 24.

Carol says she's using candy corn as a bribe to get David toilet-trained. Pat's doing all right in the daytime, even has started wearing panties to bed in the afternoon. But she absolutely soaks about four diapers a night (means one change @ two diapers each). With three or four drinks each night, what can we expect?

One night before they left, Carol curled Pat's hair. It was a rushed visit, and I thought Bob didn't even notice. Pat was up such a short time after he came home from work. But he told me the other day she looked the cutest that night that he has ever seen her. So on my next trip to Thriftway (where I saw Carol's type of curlers), I'll buy some and see if I can curl Pat's hair myself.

The other evening I heard Bob go in the bathroom, take Steve out of the tub, and spank him soundly. I asked later what had happened. He said Steve had a toy cup, and was nonchalantly pouring cups of water out of the tub onto the floor. Pat was standing there with a towel, mopping up as fast as he poured.

Eric enjoys Grandpa Lindsay's yard.

Eric has turned into as good a child (by "good," I mean easy to care for) as I could possibly want. No waking up at night, usually waits for his three meals until I've eaten, etc. He had a wonderful time last week when we visited Bob's parents.

Pat had roseola last week, with a high fever Tuesday and Wednesday. She seemed all right on Thursday, but was broken out Friday. Only inconvenience was that we'd invited a couple over for supper Friday night. The woman is three or four months pregnant, and Friday morning I had no idea whether Pat had measles or roseola. Of course we cancelled the dinner. Shirley's doctor told her it was silly to take any chances, and I thoroughly agreed.

Mike just brought me a picture he painted in school this morning, and told me a story about it: *Once there was a little girl named Jane who didn't do anything but pick flowers, but her mommy didn't want her to pick flowers. But Jane didn't have any toys to play with. Then one day her mother brought her some toys, only they were for babies, and Jane didn't like them. Then her mother brought her a gun, but that's for boys. Then her mother brought her a doll, and Jane liked that.*

It's Mike's first story.

Steve does such devilish things. An extremely simple example, yet the same type of thing happens constantly — yesterday morning he brought in the paper as I was getting breakfast. I had Pat's plate, silver, and a full glass of orange juice setting on her placemat, a stiff red plastic one. First thing I knew, Steve had casually slid the entire paper under the placemat and was getting a bang out of watching the orange juice balance precariously on top of the placemat on top of the paper. Perhaps he'll be a juggler some day.

Love, Jeanne

March 25, 1958

Dear Dad,

We're beginning to recover from Saturday night. The Barbershop Parade is a bigger night for us than New Year's Eve, you know. I went to the Parade with Nadean, my next-door neighbor. Her husband Bob was ill, so couldn't attend. Then Bob and I attended the Afterglow with Wilma and Leo Cramer. For this, members, wives, and friends go to the Savoy Hotel and sit around tables listening to all the quartets sing all over again. This ends about 1 or 1:30 a.m. Then we leave.

Lots of them stay for some woodshedding, and it turns into a whing-ding of a party. Upstairs on the 11th floor of the Savoy some Solar people were having a party. Two of the quartets were there too. Since Bob was "hosting" one of these quartets, we all (Cramers and us) went up for awhile. These two quartets sang all over again.

Since one wasn't especially good, I was beginning to get the idea I'd heard enough barbershopping for awhile. Then the Confederates, international champions last year, sang some more and redeemed the art of barbershopping.

From there (and again, we left while the party was still going strong) we brought Cramers home for chili, crackers, relishes, cheese and fruit. They went home at 1 a.m. . . . and we dropped into bed.

Doug Ecklund was christened Sunday and we were the godparents. We were due at the First Lutheran Church in east Des Moines at 10 a.m. The christening was to be in the chapel with only Ecklunds, Signe (Kelly's mother), Lindsays, and the minister, so we decided to take all four children. I called Bob E. just as we were leaving for directions on getting there. He gave us the

wrong address (Des Moines and 7th, whereas it's at 5th) and we
ended up at the Central Lutheran Church (Des Moines and 9th),
where we waited for awhile.

Finally someone there investigated and sent us back to
the right church. By that time Bob E. was out looking for us.
One thing — we met the nicest people at the Central Lutheran
Church. We decided it's the friendliest church we've ever
run across.

The minister (the right one this time) had a membership class
in the chapel to observe the baptism. Signe corralled Ecklund's
four older ones and managed nicely. Bob laid down the law to
Mike, Steve, and Pat, then sat them down in the front seat on the
other side. He held Eric during the service. The minister
commented that he hoped he baptized the right baby.

Needless to say, Mike, Steve, and Pat did not sit quietly
during the entire ceremony. I ended up holding Pat's hand quite
firmly, and the boys were told the score when we left. Bob said
we should have adopted a couple of the members of the membership class to sit between the children, but we didn't think of that
in time.

Ecklunds left yesterday. They're renting a big old house in

Eric practices standing.

Keokuk. I imag-
ine they'll be
glad to be settled,
although Kelly
wasn't eager to
move.

Each of the
three morn-
ings Bob was
in Chicago last
week, Mike and
Steve came in to
bed with me for
half an hour or
so. The first day
Mike snuggled up
close, put his arm

around me, and said, "We came in because you're all alone, and we don't want you to be lonely without Daddy." He's a nice boy.

We got along all right, but of course were very glad to see Bob when he returned. He had dinner Wednesday night with Bob Watts, a high school classmate. Bob phoned his sister Marge at least three times and talked to her for a long time, but wasn't able to see them. He brought back glowing reports of the stores and the clothes (mostly women's, but some men's) he saw in Chicago store windows. Some day we're going shopping.

Bob made the radical suggestion last night that we wait ten years before having the next baby so we could do some things like that. Sounds good!

Tomorrow morning I'm planning to visit Mike's school, the first time I will have been in the new one. I'm going to pick up my sitter at 8:30, take Mike to school, and visit 8:45-9:15, then go down to Blank Children's Hospital where I'm attending a meeting for out-of-town Guild membership drive workers 9:30-11:30. I'm going because I'm handling out-of-town publicity for them. (Theta Sigma Phi, our journalism alumnae group, handles all Guild publicity.)

From there I'm to pick up Bob for lunch, and hope we have time to buy some material at Younkers for the lining and blouse for my Easter suit. At 1:30 I have an appointment to have my hair cut and set. By 3:15 I have to be home, have taken my sitter home, and be ready to take care of Barbara Derby's four children while she has a conference with Craig's teacher. Think I'll make everything?

Steve and Pat spend most of their time outside digging in the garden now. Steve tells me what beautiful birthday cakes they make for me. Usually Pat comes in with a good share of the garden in her hair. She has a fairly decent ponytail now — for nearly five minutes after it's combed.

Love, Jeanne

April 29, 1958

Dear Dad,

I just got home — I left this morning at 8:30 for an 8:45 hair-cutting appointment at the Hotel Commodore. A Mr. James cut my hair, and I like him. He was through at 9 a.m. – what a gyp – $2 for ten minutes of clipping! Perhaps I should farm the kids out and go into the beauty business.

I had 45 minutes free with stores not even open, so I visited Ruth Webber, a friend on 59th Street, for a cup of coffee (seemed odd to see her without any of my children). Then a 9:45 meeting at Blank Hospital. I don't much like their meetings because they waste so much time. Guess I'm just not the committee-meeting type.

After that I went downtown, bought a chemise pattern (don't know what material I'll use yet). Then I picked Bob up for lunch at Johnny and Kay's, something we'd only done once or twice in the six years we've been here until this spring. I wish we could do this about once a month — makes me feel so frivolous. Anyhow, the day's been fun.

I'm beginning to miss the Hamlins more during this nice weather. I haven't had the kids out for a picnic yet. Carol and I took them all on a picnic in February last year.

Carol's life sounds fascinating. They're climbing the mountain, riding on an Old West train, etc. Her house sounds so nice, and the descriptions of the ones they're shopping for amaze me. I didn't realize that in California a swimming pool goes with lots of medium priced homes, sometimes even a guest house.

They've bought a small sports car which sounds like fun. We'd love to have an Izetta (one door in front, the cheapest, I think) or a Volkswagen (not so cheap), but certainly aren't considering getting it. Perhaps we'd better get this one paid for! Our tax refund is spent — but it was nice.

Bob's started playing tennis on Sunday mornings with Arlo Knowles. He was disgusted last Sunday — it was so cold and cloudy that they gave up, and went out for coffee. Then almost as soon as he got home, the sun came out, and the rest of the day was absolutely beautiful.

We did something different last week. Marge (Bob's sister) and her three children (18 months, 31/2, and almost 5) spent two weeks with Mother and Dad Lindsay. I wanted to see her, but Bob claimed he couldn't miss a Saturday morning meeting at Solar. Actually, I think he's too much of a coward to spend two days with seven kids. Anyhow, he took us to Ames Thursday afternoon, and we took the train to Denison, a two-hour trip.

Eric slept part of the way, and the train was nearly empty, so we had fun. A lady was sitting behind Mike. She was very nice to him, but after she bought an ice cream bar and I wouldn't let the children have any, Mike asked her all kinds of questions about it.

"Is it good?

"What flavor is it?

"Don't spill it."

Brad and Eric: Are we friends?

Finally, the woman very quietly and tactfully moved to the back of the car.

Steve and Pat, of course, had to go to the bathroom, but luckily waited until Eric was asleep. I left Mike to baby-sit while I took them clear to the back of the car. Pat was so fascinated with the trip, she barely succeeded in

Cousins Curt, Brad, Amy Milton in Grandma's kitchen.

accomplishing her mission. Mike admitted later he made a tour of the observation car while we were gone. Luckily the seats sloped inward, and Eric sleeps quietly. I hope no one noticed him there all alone. I wouldn't like to be arrested for child desertion.

Marge's youngest boy, Brad, is 18 months old and a real character. He still takes a bottle, stays in the playpen most of the time, has apparently never been expected to mind, and is still considered a baby. But he weighs 30 pounds and throws his weight (also dishes, and anything else he can grab) around correspondingly.

Whenever he was out of the playpen, little Eric (about half his size — they looked ridiculous side by side) was terrified, and would race to the other side of the room. Eric scarcely smiled the first 1 1/2 days we were there. But when Brad was in the playpen (which Eric hasn't been in for a month or so), Eric had his turn at being the kingpin. He'd actually taunt Brad. He'd crawl over to the playpen, hold toys just out of Brad's reach, and wave them at him. At that point, we didn't feel too much pity for Eric.

Incidentally, when Bob drove in Saturday night about 10 p.m., Mother said he looked more rested than she'd seen him in years!

Friday and Saturday Marge and I and the seven kids got along beautifully, but Sunday was a little more complicated. Marge and Bob don't appear to be too fond of each other. When he shows up, Marge stops expecting her kids to mind (probably because she knows it bothers Bob), and Bob gets stricter than usual. Thursday and Friday all (except Eric) had a whee of a time climbing Dad's apple tree and sitting on a big, empty gas tank out in the yard. But these things seemed dangerous to Bob, so Curt and Amy spent the day telling Marge what Uncle Bob wouldn't let them do.

It was the second time I'd left Bob overnight. The other time was when I went to a convention and left the kids with him. I wouldn't want to do this for two weeks at a time, as Marge does, but a couple of nights every eight or ten years might not be too bad.

Steve looks nicely ferocious. Craig Derby hit him over the head with our toy rake Sunday evening — made a gash just above Steve's left eyelid. He's awfully proud of his Band-Aid. I'm afraid Craig really caught it from Barbara. She gets excited. I thought it was quite fair, for about a month ago Steve hit Marcia with the same rake, gouging her knee.

Speaking of blood and guts, a glass broke with my hand in it the other day. The circular gash on my hand scared me — I'm a coward about blood. I called Bob just to get calmed down, and he sent me over to Nadean next door. She assured me it didn't amount to much.

Mike was so sweet though. He sopped up the blood while I was on the phone, watched Eric while I went next door. Then, when I came back and said I couldn't finish the dishes, he did them for me. I was impressed.

When Bob came home, Mike said, "Mommy cut her finger and she was scared, but Nadean said it wasn't anything." Mike didn't seem disapproving, just acted as if he had to put up with my eccentricities —a cross he had to bear, you might say.

Love, Jeanne

May 8, 1958

Dear Dad,

You remember Peg, my friend from college? She invited us to visit her, and I think she means it. Maybe we will some day, in spite of the resolve I made three years ago when I was seven months pregnant with Pat.

We had only Steve and Mike, and we'd just moved into our new house. We had new furniture, carpet, walls weren't messy yet, etc. Well, friends of ours spent four days with us. They had a three-year-old boy and ten-month-old twin boys, and the visit practically ruined the friendship as far as we were concerned. We decided then we should never take our children to visit anyone for more than one day, other than parents, of course.

But I've changed a lot of my ideas since then. The carpet is worn out, as are the sectionals, and the walls are grimy. The problem was that their children were the first to throw up on the carpet, wet on the sectionals, etc.

I still refuse to believe that there are many people who would enjoy having us with four small children staying with them. On the other hand, I love having company. The exception is for about six weeks after I've had a baby – then I'm a sissy – but I don't plan to be in that situation again for some time.

We haven't seen Betty and Carl since Christmas, 1956, and I'd like them to meet Eric. He has darker hair and eyes than our other children, and I think looks a little like Betty, or at least our mother's side of the family. But we can't get too eager about extra travel with all these little characters.

I asked Peg, who lives on a farm, whether she thinks she'd enjoy living in a development like we do. This is the kind of neighborhood the sociologists fuss about when they say American individualism is dying. I forget there are other people besides children, birth to ten years, and adults 25-35. At church we occasionally see older people, but even the church is mostly young.

We like our neighbors, but after spending a few days with Bob's parents, I came back wanting more privacy, and especially some trees. I have a feeling Peg would hate it here. We put up a partial six-foot fence on one side, and our neighbor on the other side works most days, so at least I can hang up clothes without having to be cheerful to someone! And sometimes I can even be out with our children only, but that is truly a rarity.

I'm not complaining. I really think I like this best for this stage when the children are small. I like borrowing from neighbors, having coffee when I have time (not regularly – our block isn't that sociable), and having someone to check with if one of the children gets an especially hard fall or cut. But when they're older, I hope we can have more space. We have no plans whatsoever of moving in less than five years, though, and may not be able to then.

One hour later. My neighbor came over, and since I can't carry on a conversation too well while I'm typing, I quit.

Bob's starting a two-week vacation next week, left over from last year. The first week we're going to his parents' place, and they're going on a vacation trip while Bob helps in their store. We've done that several times and it works out beautifully. We feel we "owe" them a week for the week Mother spent with us when Eric was born. (It's quite hard for her to do that because she works in the store all the time.) It's a vacation for Bob because the work is so different from what he does here. It actually saves us money, for we have no living expenses.

Also important, I enjoy it. I have the conveniences of home (automatic washing machine, crib, high chair, etc.) plus a pretty yard, and nothing to do except the minimum. I intend to take no clothes that need starching. Each day (and it had better be sunny) I plan to have a load of wash done by 9 a.m. When it dries I'll press whatever's necessary, and I'll have practically no other work to do.

The second week of vacation we plan to stay home. We don't

Steve, Mike, Pat in Grandpa L.'s back yard.

have our garden planted yet, and need to do some yard work. Bob hasn't mowed the yard yet. All the neighbors have, and last week the little kids were asking him why he hadn't. He told them long grass is much nicer to play in, looks better, and it's much wiser not to mow your lawn.

"Why don't you ask your father about it?" he finished.

One little girl promptly trotted home, talked to her father, and came back to tell Bob her dad doesn't like long grass. She sounded slightly disillusioned with her father. I'm sure he appreciated us.

I'm on another diet. The only way I can lose weight is to do it with someone else. After Steve was born, we had no scale, so I went next door once a week. My neighbor was interested and encouraged me, and I kept at it long enough to get down to less than I'd weighed since I was 18. But after Pat was born I never did get around to losing much.

The three months before Eric was born I managed not to gain any (I'd already gained 18 pounds at six months!) by going on a diet with an underweight friend. She gained while I lost, and we encouraged each other. But I've still wanted to lose about ten pounds since Eric was born.

His birth was discouraging – I didn't lose the 20 pounds I expected at delivery. So now another friend who's trying to lose is cooperating with me. Each Wednesday we're checking, but it's been only two weeks since we started. This vacation won't help me.

I bought a pattern for a chemise the other day and don't want to look like a barn in it. (Bob is peculiar. He likes chemises.) My pattern is fitted in front though, and has the bloused back.

Eric enjoyed the swing at Grandpa's.

I read some statistics the other day that disproved the theory that brainy women are less happy than others. Actually, I think there are just as many brainy women who have enough intelligence to know that homemaking is stimulating, and if we really want to, we can find plenty of other things to do too.

I like to read the *Ladies Home Journal*'s "How America Lives" section. The April issue story is about a woman who always wanted to be a doctor. Before she entered medical school, however, she got married, and had four children in five or six years. Her husband was a factory worker, someone who probably wouldn't ever make much money.

She decided since she wanted to have the things that go with a professional man or woman, she'd become the professional in her family. When the youngest child was in second grade, she and her husband made all sorts of sacrifices so she could go to medical school. Now she's out, the kids are mostly in high school, and she thinks her husband will change jobs in order to move to wherever she wants to practice. They'll buy a nice home there.

The article was interesting, but sounded sort of awful, too. I'm glad I'm not the brainy one in this family. It's much more convenient when it's the man who is ambitious.

Eric is still little — weighs about 16 pounds. He isn't even on the scale in the *Better Homes and Gardens Baby Book*. I'd like him at least to reach the "small" growth line.

Sometimes I wonder if Eric has a slightly nervous disposition. When we were in Arthur with Marge's kids, he didn't smile for the first two days. As I probably told you, Brad is 18 months old, weighs 30 pounds, is considered still a baby, and is a holy terror He throws things (such as china teacups into the sink). I refused to sit by him at the table because I was half afraid of him. So you can imagine what Eric thought. I didn't think we'd overprotected him, but after seeing Brad, decided our kids are pretty good to Eric.

Last fall when we had the four Hamlin children here for four days, Eric refused to eat, and was awfully unhappy. Bob says it's reasonable to assume that either he'd have to be nuts like the rest of us, or else be a nervous wreck. We're beginning to wonder if it's the latter. But he's so sweet.

Pat is outgrowing her sweetness. The neighbors still like her, but she's reached the negative stage with a rush. She toilet-trained herself when she had chickenpox, but still soaks two diapers at night. When we have nice weather, I might take her diapers off her for a week, plan to wash sheets every day, and see what happens. If she's still wetting after a week, though, I'll put her back in diapers.

Steve is a character. He's always been able to put things over on me better than Mike, because Steve can make me laugh. But he's getting a little more difficult to handle these days. He simply won't go to bed at night without being scolded, and usually gets spanked for getting up after he's in bed. He and Mike can't seem to behave together in the bathroom, and we always get into trouble over that too.

The last two nights I've put Mike and Steve to bed separately, one first one night, the other first the next night. It works better.

Love, Jeanne

May 25, 1958

Dear Dad,

It's now 2:30 p.m., and very peaceful around here. Eric and I took a sunbath for nearly an hour while the other children were napping. Then I put Eric to bed, and apparently he's asleep now. He's the sweetest little sunbather. He's almost a year old, and has been crawling all over the house for months, and seems very active. Yet so far, he stays on the blanket with me in the yard, playing with a couple of toys and chattering to me.

It's just our second sunning together, so surely before long he'll be running off all over the yard. During the last 15 minutes when I removed his shirt, pants, shoes and socks, he talked a blue streak. Apparently he couldn't quite figure out what we were doing.

Pat put me on the spot yesterday. She doesn't drink enough milk, so yesterday morning I told her if she'd drink her milk, she'd grow bigger. She gulped it down immediately and happily. BUT she then was determined to go to school with Mike.

"I drank my milk so I'm a bigger girl now. I'm going to school!"

This week Steve's Band-Aid is on his chin. Somehow he managed to fall on his Playskool bench Sunday and gash his chin. (Must have been difficult to accomplish.) He's always wearing Bob's Boy Scout cap down over his forehead, so he has to squint to see. He can't stand short-sleeved shirts, and will choose a wool one if it's in his drawer. (I finally hid those.) Now that it's warm, he still insists on wearing a jacket outside; inside, too, if I'd let him.

Steve's been naughty about bedtime with his favorite baby

sitter a couple of times. Nancy said, "What can I do? He lies
there and fusses and won't go to sleep. Then, just as I finish
scolding him, he sniffles and says, 'My, you smell pretty.'"

Pat's been somewhat of an angel compared with Steve and
Mike. However, the other day she was fussing with Eric because
he was bothering her so I told her to take her tractor into her
room, shut the door, and play. Everything was very quiet for
almost 30 minutes.

Then Steve came out, leading Pat, and said, "Mommy, look!"

Pat had gotten into a new big tube of A&D ointment and
liberally smeared it all over herself, her Elsie doll, the Playskool tractor, and the window sill, the hideabed, and worst of all,
smeared it all over her hair. I paddled her and stuck her in the
bathtub immediately and started scrubbing her, but her hair still
looks awful. It took daily showers for nearly a week to get it out.

A couple of weeks later, for no apparent reason, Pat said, "I
won't get into the grease again." And she won't because I keep it
in the top hall drawer that she can't possibly open.

While Steve was dressing this morning, he apparently fell
backwards while trying to put on a too-tight t-shirt, and hurt his
neck quite badly. He refused to sit up, barely moved, and cried
hard. He was hungry, so he drank milk and orange juice through
a straw. I was out of straws, but Nadean next door, bless her, had
some nice circus straws. We fed him peanut butter toast (his typical breakfast). Then Bob took him to Blank Hospital for an x-ray.
Three hours and $30 worth of x-rays later, they came home.

"There's nothing wrong with Steve except a bad Charley-
horse, a pulled muscle or ligament," he said. About all we can do
is apply heat and sympathize, and hope it's better in a day or two.

Yesterday morning Steve, Pat, Eric and I decided to visit
Mike's school. Steve and I took a "birthday" treat over before
Easter for Mike, and Steve behaved and had a marvelous time.
Pat has been wanting to go ever since. Steve and Pat understood
that if either of them, or Eric, made the least bit of trouble, we'd
leave immediately.

When we first went in, Pat spied an empty chair across the
room and dashed for it, while Mrs. Amick was saying over and
over, "Here, honey, you sit here." She was doubtless thinking

what a pill Pat was, and hoping she wouldn't stay long. But after Pat understood where to sit, she was nice. They were absolutely angelic for nearly 30 minutes. Even Steve! Every time the teacher asked the children a question about their workbook, Pat raised her hand and looked hopeful.

Our curly-haired Eric.

We still haven't cut Eric's hair properly. Several more people have said, "My, what a sweet little girl," which bothers me, but Bob thinks it's funny. I'm afraid Eric will start getting heat rash before long because of it. It's curling in the back and I don't like curly-headed men. Waves are all right, but not long curls!

As you know, when we entertain, I like to try new things. Most of the time, the food's edible. However, when Bob invited his boss and his wife, Jim and Margaret Stone, over for dinner last week, he had one request: "Please don't try something new, Dear. Just fix a good dinner that you know works!"

I was indignant, but agreed to go along with his request. The menu for the main course was totally unmemorable. However, I decided I needed to finish the meal with a flourish. I'd fix a really great and very special dessert. Surely no great risk there.

I searched through my dessert recipes. I'd made cheesecake several times, with great results. Maybe a different kind of cheesecake this time?

I found a recipe for a beautiful strawberry-almond cheesecake. The cheesecake I'd made before was the kind you bake. This one was to be refrigerated, and plain gelatin was one of the ingredients. I hadn't used gelatin before, other than Jell-O.

I've always thought if a recipe calls for a small amount of herbs or spices, using more must be even better. I saw that the cheesecake ingredients included one packet of plain gelatin. I realized this was to make the cheesecake set up as it was supposed to do. I thought how terrible it would be if my dessert was runny when I served it. How to prevent such a catastrophe? Add

an extra packet of gelatin, of course. So I did. The cheesecake
set up beautifully. With the strawberry-almond mixture on top, it
was worthy of a *Better Homes & Gardens* photo shoot.

The conversation flowed smoothly as we ate that very dull
first course. I cleared the table, and brought in the beautiful
cheesecake. Of course something so lovely must be served in
front of our guests. I carefully placed pieces on each dessert
plate and breathed a sigh of relief. It was definitely not runny.

We started to eat this gorgeous dessert. We started chewing.
And chewing. And chewed some more. Our guests were looking
a little startled.

My beautiful dessert seemed to be filled with little chunks of
rubber tire – not quite the effect I wanted. To my chagrin, that
extra gelatin had morphed into rubber.

So much for my innovative cooking efforts.

We've worried quite a bit about Mike, and Bob and I keep
having discussions on what we should do different with him. His
teacher's biggest criticism is that he doesn't listen as he should,
and she suggested we tell him something once, and expect him
to hear it. We've been trying. Of course the difficulty there is that
it's probably partly my fault. I still talk too fast, and sometimes
it's hard for them to understand me.

Actually, almost everyone I know has more trouble with
the first one, largely because we expect too much, I think, and
haven't developed much tolerance yet. Mike is one of the younger ones in his class, and we've already assured his teacher that
if she thinks he should be kept back a year, we're all for it. (Bob
was too young all through school and still feels strongly that he
was cheated.) But she says there's no reason to think about that
for Mike, this year at least. We'll see how he does on reading
next year in first grade.

It almost seems to be the style here to keep the kids back a
year in the lower grades. So many of the children around here
seem to do it. Doesn't quite jibe with all the propaganda on the
state of education in this country, in which the evils of automatic
passing on to the next grade are frequently discussed.

Love, Jeanne

June 17, 1958

Dear Dad,

We thought we'd see you by now. Are you all right? Have any of the tornadoes been near you? Have you gotten lots of rain?

Speaking of rain — I was down in our garden early this morning "plowing" it with my fingers. We went to Arthur Sunday. Mother sent back some flower plants with us, marigolds and others, which I didn't recognize. Yesterday morning Mike and I planted them in the empty part of our garden. He did a great job, the best he's ever cooperated with gardening.

But last night we had a cloudburst that flooded the garden again. This morning there wasn't a sign of most of the plants we'd so carefully put in. I found them under about three inches of black dirt. I think I rescued most of them, but they're so muddy they may not survive. The cucumbers had come up nicely yesterday, and they also disappeared. I found some of them. I never saw so many or such big fish worms in my life. Too bad I couldn't get them to you — and I wish we could go fishing together.

After the storm we all drove downtown to pick up Bob's new suit at Penny's. We saw the most beautiful rainbow we'd seen for quite a while. Bob told the children about the pot of gold at the end of it. First we thought we saw it (the end of the rainbow) in the brick yard out here, but as we went on downtown it moved to the 14th floor of the Equitable Life Insurance building. Mike and Steve were a trifle dubious about the pot of gold story, but Bob almost had me convinced.

We've had a couple of hot days – time to turn on the sprinkler. They always have a wonderful time playing in the water.

*No air condition-
ing – but hot
Iowa days are
managed nicely
with a sprinkler.*

*First, you get
ready – and here
it comes!*

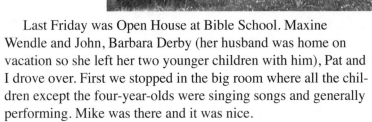

Last Friday was Open House at Bible School. Maxine
Wendle and John, Barbara Derby (her husband was home on
vacation so she left her two younger children with him), Pat and
I drove over. First we stopped in the big room where all the children except the four-year-olds were singing songs and generally
performing. Mike was there and it was nice.

Then I went over to Steve's class. Last year I thought I was
thrilled with Mike because he was the first one to attend Bible
School, then to start sschool. Now I've decided each one will be
just as thrilling.

When I first walked in, several of the children were stretched
out on the floor. Steve was standing by his teacher, and she was
saying he'd be the rain and the other little boy would be the sun.
Then they sang a song about the seeds in the ground and how
the sun and the rain make them grow. Then Steve and the other

Such a big candle for Eric's first birthday!

one ran around the children (who were the seeds) until they got up.

After that they played some finger games. Then the teacher said they'd say their Bible verse. First Steve said it, then they all did together. I wish you could have seen him, dressed in his short-sleeved white shirt and dark blue short pants, standing there looking completely angelic (you could almost see his halo) as he said, "Be kind one to another." I couldn't help but remember all the times in our yard when he's fighting with Mike, teasing Pat, etc., but at the moment butter couldn't possibly have melted in his mouth.

Later his teacher told me how cooperative he'd been, how much they liked him, and how well she thought he'd do in school. And I told her what Steve said when he got home from Bible School the first day, "I colored, we sang songs, and I SAT ON MY TEACHER'S LAP!"

He probably told her she had a pretty dress on nearly every day, or some such blarney. Bob says if Steve gets a young teacher in kindergarten, he'll probably give her a thrill with all his flattery. He rather hopes Steve gets an older one who won't be taken in by all that, and who will teach him something.

Yesterday Jean Roseberry and her mother came over for tea and chocolate angel food cake. Steve walked over to me and said quietly, but just loud enough so Jean could hear, "Jean sure is pretty, isn't she?"

Love, Jeanne

June 26, 1958

Dear Dad,

The dishes aren't done — it's 8:15 a.m., one load of wash is in, and Mike, Steve and Pat are all drawing and coloring at the table. So this seems a better time to write you, although the table is a bit crowded. Where will we put Eric when he starts drawing?

Each child has drawn a picture to send you, and Mike and Steve have told me what to write on theirs. The other day Mike asked me if I'd ever been in a tornado so I told him a little about ours. Naturally he was impressed. He was telling Steve all about it this morning, which explains Steve's picture of a tornado on Grandpa Warren's farm.

We had a lovely day yesterday. Men were laying a telephone cable in the ground up at the corner, so about 11 a.m. we went up to watch — Mike, Steve, Pat, Eric, and Marcia Derby. (I'd gotten Marcia's mother's permission to take her across the street.) Soon Pam from next door showed up. Then Mark came trotting over. He's three, and of course not supposed to cross the street.

I asked Mark if his mother knew he was there. He solemnly nodded his head. But he sat down and sucked his thumb all the time he was there, which convinced me he was feeling guilty. (He seems to suck his thumb mostly when he's been naughty.) I didn't take him home because he might have been telling the truth, and because it would have been a major undertaking to get all the other children back and forth across the street.

Finally, he stood up suddenly, mumbled, "I'd better go home," and took off. Pam (10) took charge of the others including Eric, and I took Mark across the street and sent him home.

Marta, his six-year-old sister, conveyed the wonderful news

to her mother that Mark had been across the street. Whereupon Mark got a good spanking, I understand.

The rest of us stayed a while longer, watching the ditch digging machine and the man laying the cable plus the terrifically noisy gadget that tamps the earth down on top of it. Pat made quite an impression on the men running it, mainly because she got so excited. We all made exceptional sidewalk superintendents, I thought. Finally we went home to lunch.

After the others were in bed yesterday afternoon, Mike changed Myrtle's water (our turtle), washed her bowl, and fed her. Then he made instant pudding and washed all his dishes afterward. But a tragedy occurred. When he got ready to eat his dessert last night he discovered it hadn't set. I can't imagine why instant pudding wouldn't turn out right, unless he beat it too long. I would much rather have had something I made fail. It'll be fun when he learns to read well enough to follow recipes by himself.

Steve and I covered an old cookbook yesterday with heavy plastic material. We used wallpaper paste which really sticks. Steve cut up the left-over scraps of plastic and pasted them on the Indian book you gave him last fall. He said he was making feathers.

Eric still can't walk but has learned to climb. While I was attending the convention last week, he shocked Mrs. Thompson, our sitter, by insisting on climbing on top of the desk. Right now he's lying on our hi-fi set, and I must go get him down. It's ridiculous to learn to climb before you can walk. To make it worse, he can't get back down from anything and is forever getting stuck on top of something.

Steve and Pat have finally started using soap when they wash their hands. They're so thrilled every time that they come running, holding up their hands, saying, "Smell them, Mommy." Luckily we use nice-smelling soap.

Last weekend Bob's boss, Jim Stone, took us out to see his new boat. The children enjoyed playing by the lake, and Eric liked sitting on the boat with me.

Convention was fun. Here's a short rundown. Last Wednesday morning, Mike, Steve, Eric, and I met Gladys Hearst from

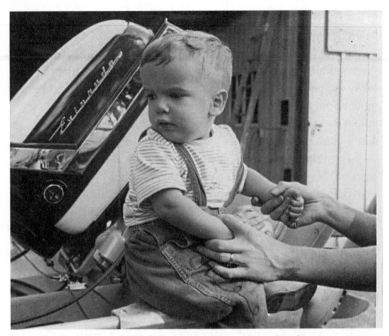

How about Eric for Jim's boat figurehead?

Cedar Falls at the airport at 9 a.m., took her out to Drake University, and returned to the airport to meet Elly Wright at 10 to take her to Drake. I had decided to take all four children to show them off, even though it didn't seem too professional. Gladys is a good friend and had never seen Eric, and I wanted her to meet him. Elly is national publicity chairman for Theta Sigma Phi, and I'd written her several times in my role as public relations chairman. But Wednesday morning Pat woke up with a fever, so I had to leave her with Nadean Phillips. When we took Elly to Drake, the three boys and I went in for a little while, so they would know where I was when I'd say I was going to convention.

Meredith Publishing Company sponsored the Thursday luncheon at the Wakona Country Club here. We had a circus theme with wonderful decorations including a little merry-go-round on the table where hot bouillon was served when we first went in. It was a buffet featuring the pictured salads in the July *Better Homes & Gardens*. We chose the one we wanted. I was toastmistress so got to sit at the head table and introduce Hugh

Curtiss, editor of *BH&G*.

When I got home at midnight, Bob informed me Mike had the mumps! Pat had also had a fever all day. Bob hadn't told me when I was home at 3 p.m. because he could see no reason to worry me, bless him. He's awfully nice.

Monday evening, when we thought both Mike and Pat had mumps, Bob took them over to the doctor. The doctor said it wasn't mumps at all, just a slight infection of the glands. Mike's been all right since, and I think Pat's all over it too.

Bob was wonderful about taking care of our family during the convention. The house didn't even get terribly messed up. But Sunday he asked me if I was looking for a new project. If so, he had a suggestion — why not make my next project the Lindsays? And for the next two months I'm taking it easy.

Bob even made a cake Saturday morning. The kids wouldn't eat it, but that wasn't his fault. He found a package of pineapple cake mix. On the package it suggested mixing chocolate with half of it and making a marble cake. Bob said he went up and down the neighborhood trying to borrow chocolate squares, but couldn't find any, so ended up just dumping some cocoa in the batter. Apparently the children don't care for pineapple and chocolate mixed (neither do I, to be perfectly honest). But I did appreciate his making the cake.

We haven't heard from you for ages. Are you all right? I thought you were going to visit us? We're disappointed that you haven't.

Is there any chance that Cleora would like to come with you? We could manage a separate bedroom for her, without any children in it, I think, if the rest of us doubled up. Of course we'd love to have her. I probably won't write her, unless you write saying she might come, in which case I'll send an official invitation.

Love, Jeanne

July 1, 1958

Dear Dad,

We were happy you called last Thursday. How long will harvesting take? Surely you can visit us soon, can't you?

It's raining nice and gently with occasional thunder this morning. All four children were outside playing, but Pat and Eric came in. Mike and Steve are running around, and Mike just came to the door to tell me Steve sat down in the water. Obviously he's having fun.

Mike got sick again last Thursday afternoon. We took him to the doctor Saturday for he hadn't been able to keep anything down for two days. Dr. Brindley gave him a shot of penicillin. He said if Mike wasn't better by Sunday morning, we should take him to the hospital to have some tests done. Vomiting and headaches can mean almost anything, of course, but he thought it was probably just an infected throat. I guess it was, for Mike's much better now – about well, I'd say. Apparently it was hard for him to start eating again, but he is now.

We learned Saturday that our doctor, Dr. Brindley, was quitting his practice Sunday morning. This week I think he's starting to study psychiatry at the State University of Iowa. We were disappointed for we like him so much. You remember him, don't you? Last fall he had a heart attack and didn't practice for a couple of months, then apparently took on his entire work load again. He ran on the Democratic ticket for county coroner in the primary election. On the news Friday night his withdrawal as a candidate was announced, so all this must have happened suddenly.

Dr. Brindley told us he decided he'd like to live long enough to see his three children grow up. He's about 35, and his children are aged 4-8. According to his doctors, he'd have to quit his strenuous general practitioner work to do this. He said he'd probably practice psychiatry in Iowa City or another college town.

We hope he'll be happy. We wonder, though, for he seems to have very little patience with hypochondriacs, and psychiatry doesn't seem like quite the ideal field for him. He bragged to the skies the doctor who is taking over his practice, so we'll probably continue to go over there.

Steve played in bed the other afternoon, and generally misbehaved, refusing to go to sleep. I'd been lying out in the sun for awhile, then came in and took a shower. Finally I lay down with Steve, with the firm intention of swatting him if he so much as blinked an eye. But he leaned toward me, sniffed, grinned, and said, "Mommy, you smell dee-wicious." What can I do?

Pat came in last night asking for her "glove." After several questions, I discovered that Janice was going to play ball with her, and Pat wanted a catcher's mitt. And we didn't think even Mike needed one yet!

Friday night we heard the Danish National Orchestra play, a Civic Music Association concert, and enjoyed it tremendously. They opened by playing the "Star Spangled Banner," then the Danish national anthem which is beautiful. The sad part was how surprised the audience seemed to be at hearing our national anthem. No one seemed to know whether to clap or not when it was over, and the flag in the theater was dirty. Patriotism doesn't seem to be especially stylish here anymore, does it? I've heard people who've traveled to Europe mention what a tremendous difference they find in other countries. People are much more obviously patriotic there.

Pam Phillips came over last week when I was making rolls. I gave her a hunk that she kneaded, then put to rise in a separate pan beside mine. She came back in the afternoon, and we each made cinnamon rolls. After they were baked, she came over and frosted hers, then took them home for supper.

Bob came home as she was doing her frosting, and had some comments to make. Pam's little pan of rolls turned out better than mine! Pam's mother, Nadean, works three or four days a week, so Pam comes over here occasionally. She's 10, and we like her so much, as I've probably told you.

I guess I'll never be a great mathematician. Mr. Oppenheimer wouldn't care to have me as his first assistant. Last night I spent the evening, while Bob was at Barbershop practice, messing with our financial records. I added up the amounts we'd spent for shelter, food, clothing, recreation, etc., during the first six months of this year, then divided it by six to get the average per month. Then I figured the percentage of Bob's take-home pay spent on each item. Everything looked lovely and I was eager to show it to Bob. THEN I added up the percentages, and we had spent 121 percent of his pay! Yet we're not in debt except for our mortgage. Bob still insists I keep the books. I think it must cater to his need to feel superior.

We're enjoying our hi-fi so much, far more than I ever did TV. Speaking of TV, though, our set has been giving us trouble. So a couple of weeks ago Bob decided to fix it. He got behind it while I kept the kids away and attempted to keep Eric from trying to chew up the spare parts. Finally Bob emerged to admit that he seemed to have broken the picture tube. Aren't we lucky that we both have enough sense, or enough inborn laziness, that we don't often try to be do-it-yourselfers?

Pat just came running with a shocked expression, saying, "Look, Mommy, look what Steve did." It's been raining all day, and Steve has an old rag outside. I was watching him for a little while — he was playing in a puddle with the rag, and I could see no harm in it. But just now Pat was standing inside looking out through the screen door. Somehow Steve managed to throw the sopping wet rag at her hard enough for the mud to make a lovely screen design on her face.

Pat gets so upset at these things that all three boys love to bother her. Eric goes absolutely ecstatic over pulling her pigtails. She fusses, tosses her head, and gets so indignant that he practically rolls with laughter.

Love, Jeanne

July 15, 1958

Dear Dad,

We visited Gladys and Chuck Hearst in Cedar Falls Saturday and had a wonderful time. They have a beautiful farm and the children loved it. We wish you lived closer — it's a shame they see a farm so seldom. Gladys and Chuck call their place Maplehearst Farm because of the thousands of maples which Chuck's great-grandfather planted when he came there. He planted the seeds in furrows, and a century later, they're mighty pretty.

They have a big collie named Sue, who terrified Steve at first (he's deathly afraid of all dogs), but Sue was so gentle and friendly that soon even Steve had made friends with her. The pigs had lots of little ones which seemed to interest Mike the most.

They also liked the ducks, which Gladys said should be chased because they needed the exercise. We didn't quite believe her though — no animal or fowl really likes to be frightened.

A tenant family live in a house right across from Gladys and Chuck. They

Steve and Pat enjoyed talking to the calf.

Next thing we know, they'll be driving that tractor.

have four children including two boys about 12 and 14 who were exceptionally nice to our children. One brought a calf out for them to pet. Another gave Mike a ride on the tractor – which we don't ordinarily quite approve of because it's too dangerous for a child to be on a tractor, don't you think?

Gladys had fixed a dinner of foods she thought the children would like — hamburgers, green beans, mashed potatoes, etc. For dessert she fixed Jell-O, knowing they like that. But she's a very interesting cook, and couldn't resist fixing it up a little.

She used four different colors of Jell-O, which she allowed to set, then chopped up into cubes. She folded all of these into whipped cream and called it Rocky Road Dessert. By the time we were ready for dessert, Pat and Eric were asleep, and the neighbor boy wouldn't touch the Jell-O. Gladys said she might as well have fixed us an exotic cream puff dessert.

Hearsts are apparently quite active in the Democratic party. When Estes Keefaufer was campaigning for president three or four years ago in Iowa, he spent a night at their house. So Saturday Eric slept in the "Keefaufer bed." You don't think any of those Democratic ideas will rub off on him, do you?

Remember when Betty told us that before she got her

automatic washing machine, the children of the neighborhood loved to watch her use her wringer washer because they'd never seen one? We ran into something even odder Saturday. Our children's favorite object was Gladys' pop-up garbage can. We don't have one because of our garbage disposal.

Gladys churns butter regularly. She had it ready to go Saturday, and Steve and Mike churned it. It was a churn just like Mother used, and they were intrigued. The buttermilk was good too.

We took the children to the Fourth of July Sheldahl picnic. Sheldahl is not far from Des Moines. They enjoyed the rides, and we listened to Governor Loveless speak.

Eric has been sick so we've met our new doctor now. Last Thursday night, Eric had trouble breathing so we were afraid he was having an attack of asthma. Apparently it was bronchitis, which he had last winter. I took him to the doctor Friday and again Monday.

Monday was the first time Pat had met the doctor. When I said, "Pat, this is Dr. Johnson," she looked up, smiled shyly, shook her head violently, and said, "I not sick . . . not any more."

Friday Dr. Johnson gave Steve his yearly check-up, and he was fine. But with all the enthusiasm of a young doctor just starting out in practice, Dr. Johnson weighed and measured Steve. Then he carefully filled out a growth chart for him at the same time, mumbling a little apologetically that Dr. Brindley didn't especially believe in this sort of thing.

Yesterday I was amused to discover that apparently Dr. Johnson is already losing some of these lofty ideas. He checked Mike over thoroughly, but neglected to bother with a growth chart.

Love, Jeanne

August 7, 1958

Dear Dad,

I just heard Steve crying pathetically so I rushed outside to investigate. Richie from next door was talking to him several houses away from here. When I asked what was wrong, Rich said, "He fell out of the tree house . . ." (and Steve cried harder), "but he's not hurt — he's not bleedin' or nothin'." At that, Steve quit crying, Rich told him to come along, and Steve turned around and followed Rich back to the tree house.

Have I told you about the tree house? The only tree we have around here is behind the first house at the end of the block — five houses away from here. Some of the older boys built a platform in it. Mike helped, and they all have a wonderful time playing there.

Mike and Mark H. collaborate.

I don't think Pat can get up in it by herself, but sometimes the older ones help her up. One night

Mike works at the finishing touches.

when I went to call her in to bed, I found her up in the tree house, crying hard. Libby (7) had put her up, but couldn't get her down. Pat was stuck there until I came. Libby was quite apologetic.

A tragedy occurred Tuesday — Myrtle passed on. And what a way to die. I was a little shook up when it happened. You see, Eric discovered her, and he was too much for Myrtle. When I found him holding her, I took her away from him, and was shocked to see that her shell was broken. When Bob came home that night, she was dead.

Bob examined Myrtle and discovered that Eric had squeezed half of her horribly. And I always prided myself on teaching the children to be nice to animals. I still remember how horrified I was when I was 4, and cousin Jack Donaldson, 3, visited us and mistreated the cats. But to get back to Myrtle, Mike, Steve and I carefully buried her the next day, in a strawberry Jell-O box in our backyard. She was the turtle Hamlins left here when they went to California.

Bob and I waxed our car Saturday in Arthur. It needed it badly for we never had waxed it. It was porcelainized when we bought it, but you can imagine the condition the finish was in. The car looks redder now.

I took Mike and four friends out to Riverview last Wednesday to celebrate his sixth birthday, rather than having the usual birthday party. Another mother went with us, and brought along her little girl, so we actually had six children. We got along beautifully, but were exhausted that night.

It's a park with all kinds of children's rides. The most nerve-wracking was the race car in which an adult had to ride with the children because the cars have the regular gas feed and operate rather like a real car. It's not supposed to bump into the other cars either.

First thing to do is ride the horse at the park.

We managed to talk all of the children out of riding it except Mike and Mark Green. I sat in the middle with my foot very close to the brake pedal. Mark handled the steering wheel (with me grabbing it when necessary), and Mike operated the gas pedal. The boys enjoyed it.

Most complicated part of the afternoon was when we bought pop and each child had to decide which kind he wanted.

We bought Mike a rifle just like the one Steve got for Christmas. It's saving lots of arguments. Normally we don't think they both need to have the same thing, but this seemed different. Mike has wanted one for more than a year.

We're wondering if you and Cleora will be visiting us soon.

Love, Jeanne

August 19, 1958

Dear Dad,

We can't visit you this year. Solar decided the three weeks
vacation had to be taken all at once, something about taking
three weeks to unwind entirely, or some such rot. We definitely
didn't want to take the entire vacation this summer for several
reasons. Mainly, we have no vacation money until our car is paid
for this fall, plus the fact that Eric wouldn't be great sport for
much traveling.

Also, Solar has been cutting back terrifically. They're down
to 1400 men from a high of 3600 two or three years ago. They
completely eliminated Bob's Industrial Engineering department
a year ago, laid off almost the entire group of 27, and gave Bob
an entirely different job. Anyhow, although he feels pretty secure
so far, he likes the idea of having two or three weeks of vacation
pay left in case they do "terminate" him. I guess this is a nice
word for "lay off," which in turn, in my vocabulary, is a nice
word for "fire."

Eric still doesn't walk. Thank heaven the other two his age
on the block have just now started walking a little. Eric will be
15 months old September 1. If the others had been early walkers,
starting at nine or ten months, I'd probably be frantic by now,
especially since we took him to a foot specialist twice last winter
because his feet turn out a little too much. But we're convinced
he just isn't interested in walking. There's nothing wrong with
his feet now.

Eric is so sweet – by far the most loving one we've had
(when he's in the mood, I mean). We have a ten-year-old girl,
Pam, next door south and a twelve-year-old girl, Janice, north,

Eric loves to pet Cinder, Pam P.'s dog.

and between them they spoil him terrifically. He loves it, and I like him to get the attention. Also, they take care of him an hour or so a day. I'll miss them when school starts.

Do you suppose Mike will be able to visit you for a few days in the summer when he's a little older? We seem to have to scold him so much for tearing around and being generally rambunctious.

On a farm Mike is a different boy. Sunday, friends of Mother and Dad's had us out to their farm for dinner. He behaved beautifully and had lots of fun, probably because he could run around and not hurt anything. He likes the animals so much. Any time Mike talks about what he'll do when he grows up, he says he's going to be a farmer and live with Grandpa Warren.

Mike's school starts next week. I'd better get busy and check his jeans and shirt supply and get an order in to Sears if necessary. It must be a lot more simple getting a boy ready for school than getting all those dresses for a girl. The Catholic school here won't let the boys wear jeans, even first graders! Sounds perfectly ridiculous to me. They seem a little young for the no-jeans-equals-a-gentleman theory.

Love, Jeanne

August 24, 1958

Dear Dad,

I'm thrilled that you and Cleora are getting married this fall.
When I got your letter, I immediately phoned Bob and was
practically incoherent as I told him he was going to have a step-
mother-in-law. When I told Mike and Steve that Grandpa Warren
is getting married, they clapped their hands and yelled — but
they clap their hands and yell at everything.

So you haven't told Betty and Carl yet. Surely they'll be
happy, too. We were thinking we might drive to Manhattan Labor
Day to see Betty and Carl, partly because you'll be there. But
since you'll be here two weeks later and, as Betty's letter yesterday didn't sound as thrilled as we thought she should (after all,
think of the six lovely people offering to spend the weekend with
her), we've about decided to stay home. Actually, with the heat,
and the way these four characters do not adjust well to traveling, we were looking hard for a reason not to go. We still might,
though, for I'd like to see them. Last time was Christmas, 1956,
and I want them to meet Eric.

Mike still hasn't lost any teeth. We're wondering when he
will, and are prepared to play the good fairy.

Eric discovered this morning that, by climbing first into Pat's
chair, he can climb right up onto the table. He's thrilled . . .
I'm not.

Eric still isn't walking. Pam and Janice have talked him into
standing alone for a second or two a few times. Once I think he
even forgot himself to the great extent of taking a step. Maybe
he'll celebrate his second birthday by walking. We still don't
think it's because of his feet though, for they turn out very little

Why walk when there's always someone to carry me?

now. He just is slow about walking.

A month ago I started wondering if we might be able to get a bigger house. I was reading ads like crazy, going out to look at houses, etc., but I'm completely out of the mood now. We priced several older homes on acreages, houses I'm not sure I'd take if they offered an even trade for ours, and the prices were around $22,000-$24,000. The ones I really liked were $30,000 or so.

The reason I keep saying "I" instead of "we" is because Bob was mostly going along just to humor me. He has better sense than to try to borrow $20,000 or so for just another house. The gist of it is, the houses I like are so expensive that if we could possibly buy one, we couldn't afford anything else at all that would be fun. Phooey!

Bob has started looking at sport cars. At first it depressed me. I got worried that we might spend all our money for another car except what we need for the bare necessities. I want to fix up the basement, and buy some "gadgets" (radio, lamp, etc.) that we haven't been able to afford because of paying for this car.

Bob is a very diplomatic man. When he casually mentioned his sport car "shopping" was exactly the same as my house shopping, I came around. And now, darn it, we've looked at enough foreign cars to make me want one.

Yesterday Mike, Steve and Pat were a credit to their father . . . too bad he didn't see them. A friend took us and her children over to the wading pool. As we were leaving, we saw a beautiful red MG convertible and all three children ran ahead of us (hers weren't the least bit interested). All three stood in a row beside the MG, oohed and aahed, reverently touched the upholstery, etc.

Seriously, neither one of us is even hoping to buy one, for quite a long time anyhow. Maybe we could put the kids to work to pay for it.

Pat's looking especially lovely now — not only are her teeth black, as usual (she's chipped them even more this summer), but she also has a startling shiner. She sat in a cardboard box last Saturday on the back step, then rolled over the side in it. Her nose bled for a while, and Bob suggested cheerfully when he got home that perhaps it was broken. He decided it wasn't, but half her cheek up under her eye has been greenish-black all week.

Louis Armstrong played at the Val Air a couple of weeks ago. We considered going, but for the second time decided to stay home and spend the money for a record. So we got a sitter the night he was here, then went shopping for the record. We did the same thing last winter when he was in Des Moines. This one has, among other things, "When the Saints Go Marching In." I'd like a 331/3 LP record consisting entirely of different arrangements of that to play while I'm doing housework. It should speed me up considerably.

Last week Mike, with the help of a couple of other boys,

made a fort by nailing a huge box to the ground in the back yard. It was the box our TV came in 1 1/2 years ago. It's been in the basement with junk in it, but my neighbor and I finally went to the junk yard last week and dumped it. Mike got the box.

He decided he'd like to sleep in it that night, and, wonder of wonders, also decided he'd like Steve in with him. They went to bed about 7:30 with just enough room for the two of them to be wedged in very close to each other, like sardines. It was miraculous, but they actually got along without fussing for 40 minutes. (Normally they fight all the time they're together.) Then for 20 minutes or so they bickered, and came in a couple of times with various complaints.

Finally at 8:30 Bob went out to find Steve pulling up grass to throw at Mike. He sent Steve in, of course, and we both thought that's what he really wanted anyhow. We didn't hear anything from Mike again until at 9:30 we took a flashlight out to check on him. He was still awake and looking a trifle serious. He said he was fine, but when I reminded him that he was welcome to come in any time he wanted to, he said he guessed he would right then. He was actually sweet about it.

Mike's had a lot of fun playing in his cardboard fort in the daytime since then. He's even suggested once or twice he might sleep in it again, but we told him he'd better wait until next year. The box is about to fall down now, but Mike still loves it. It would be nice if we could get him a little tent next summer.

Love, Jeanne

September 20, 1958

Dear Dad,

Will we see you and Cleora this weekend?

We're trying to get our house painted. I was going to finish the primer coat today but it rained, which is very frustrating. I'm also waiting for the washer repairman, for our washer quit last Friday. He promised he'd be here yesterday, but still hasn't shown up.

Bob left Sunday night for a week in Chicago attending a school to which Solar sent him. He'll come back Friday night or Saturday, be home two weeks, then go back for another week. We're lonely.

Eric complicates the painting. Would you like to take him home with you for a week? Or better yet, why don't you stay a week and take care of him while I paint?

Eric is downstairs now playing with Steve. We still keep the gate fastened so he won't fall downstairs, but he loves to go down himself when I let him. He still doesn't walk, just doesn't seem interested. He's very efficient at crawling though.

Mike is enjoying first grade a lot. He brings home two or three papers every day. If the paper is done right, the teacher draws a happy face on it. I haven't seen the other kind yet, but Mike says if it's wrong, she draws a frowning face.

We're eager to see you.

Love, Jeanne

October 27, 1958

Dear Dad and Cleora,

It's so nice to write to both of you. We're all delighted that you two decided to marry each other.

You now have the lispingist grandson ever — Steve fell on the front step yesterday, smashing his upper middle tooth out. Rather, it was left hanging with the entire root exposed (rather gory and bloody), and the dentist pulled it on out an hour later.

The tooth next to it is loosened, but should tighten up. However, it undoubtedly will turn black.

The whole thing was almost harder on Mike than on Steve. At first I couldn't understand why Mike wasn't more sympathetic . . . then realized his problem. Mike's had a loose tooth for some time. Matter of fact, the permanent tooth has grown in behind it, something the dentist says is perfectly all right. Mike can't get the loose tooth out. And now his little brother would be visited first by the tooth fairy who trades money for teeth.

After Bob and Steve left for the dentist's office, Mike practically refused to eat supper because he was trying so hard to get his tooth out. He had a washcloth ready, because he tells me gums always bleed a little when a tooth comes out.

Mike wanted to call Janice over. Janice is the 12-year-old next door who has pulled a tooth or two for most of the children in the neighborhood. I talked him into waiting until today to ask Janice. He never did get the tooth out.

Of course Steve hurt pretty bad when he fell, but Bob said he was awfully good at the dentist's. Steve didn't cry at all, although the dentist seemed rather shaky. We decided dentists don't come up against emergencies often (this was Sunday evening), and just aren't used to the blood and messiness.

Steve tried to reassure the dentist a little, Bob said. Steve told the dentist that it really didn't hurt much. He felt pretty good when he got home although Bob expected trouble in the night or today when the light anesthetic wore off. But so far Steve's been fine.

Steve hasn't eaten anything yet. He drank some milk, but that's all. He seems to be getting hungry now, and I'm fixing fish for lunch which he loves and which should be easy to eat.

Steve looks both pathetic and funny. His lips are swollen a lot and his gums are a mess. But he talks so cute. I'm afraid I laughed a little with him last night, but of course won't any more. I didn't realize children lisp when a tooth or two is missing.

The dentist says there should be no trouble now. The other teeth won't grow into the opening, and the permanent ones should come in 11/2 years or so.

Mark from up the street came in to play this morning. Most of the time he was the doctor with Pat the nurse and Steve the patient.

Will Warren and Cleora Kluss Loughridge – married October 10, 1958.

Bob got back to painting yesterday — did about half the south side of the house. We still have the doors to do.

Cleora, please send me your sizes and preferences — gloves, slips (do you prefer nylon or otherwise?), sweaters (could you use a cardigan for instance?), blouses. When is your birthday?

4 p.m. At 11:20 this morning Steve discovered he could eat. His first food was raw potato! Bob phoned at about that time. We agreed we wouldn't worry much more about little Steven.

Guess what? We bought a blue used TR-2 sports car. Bob is thrilled, and I must admit, I am too. And so are the children. We all fit in it. There's no room for a real back seat, but it has a little ledge where the back seat would be. Mike, Steve, and Pat all fit there, and Eric sits on my lap in the bucket seat in the front.

Saturday night we took all four children over to the church for chiliburgers and were surprised to discover some of them ate something. I fed Eric first, but not the others. Even though we know the others normally won't eat at all when they're out, let alone something "different" like chiliburgers, we decided this

They love our TR-2.

would be their supper. At 50¢ each, the price wasn't too bad, especially when you consider that it was Bob's class putting on the supper to make money. We felt a trifle obligated.

Anyhow, for the first time in his life, Mike ate pie, a whole piece of it, plus half his burger. Steve and Pat didn't touch the burgers, but Steve cleaned up his pie as well as Pat's. He was shocked to find that we'd let him eat pie even though he ate nothing else.

Last week I made Pat an empire waistline dress of corduroy. She thinks it's pretty although she and Steve agreed it looks like a nightgown. I hope to buy her some red leotard stockings to wear with it.

You asked about Christmas ideas for the kids. Steve said the other day that he'd sure like to have a tractor. All the ones they had are broken. The nice one you gave them a couple of years ago at Christmas, Dad, lost a wheel completely last month. It lasted pretty well, I'd say. Mike wants cowboy stuff more than anything. I think we'll buy him a pair of "Bootsters." These are leather uppers to buckle over regular shoes which are much cheaper than boots and easier on his feet, and he likes them. He'd love a cowboy shirt but they're probably too expensive. He wants cowboy gloves too.

As I told you, we're getting Pat a 12 inch Tiny Tears doll, so anything to go with it is perfect — or any Playskool or other toy clerks recommend for 3-year-olds. Eric would love an easy-to-operate top or perhaps a Playskool toy. Just use your own judgment.

A couple of weeks ago I took Eric to the doctor. He was almost 17 months old and still not walking. I sat down and Eric stood beside me.

"Aren't you walking yet, Eric?" Dr. Johnson asked. And Eric walked over to him!

He's been walking ever since. Now he thinks it's great sport to walk around and around in circles until he gets so dizzy he falls over. Just now Pat is on the rocking horse and he's been going round and round her.

Love, Jeanne

December 1, 1958

Dear Dad and Cleora,

We enjoy your letters very much. Thank you for your gift ideas, Cleora. We just about have our shopping done... that is, if Sears Roebuck comes through with what we've ordered. It's strange that both Bob and I come from small towns, yet probably do more catalog ordering now than we ever did.

We hired a sitter Saturday afternoon and went downtown — the stores were packed already. We bought wool material for a dress for me. I made a sheet dress today to see if the pattern fits, and plan to start the dress tomorrow. Tomorrow night I want to start working on clothes for Pat's new Christmas doll. It'll be the first time I've made real doll clothes from a pattern, and I think it'll be fun. Another mother told me she doesn't think a girl really plays with doll clothes much before she's 8, but if Pat doesn't like these, I will! It's a 12" baby doll that takes a bottle and cries real tears.

We had a lovely Thanksgiving Day, except for about an hour in the morning. We practically ruined it by deciding to take pictures for our Christmas cards that day. The minister opened the church for us, and lent us four choir robes. I made white covers for four books with "Noel" on them, handed them to the children, and told them to look angelic. They didn't. To make matters worse, we discovered later the camera wasn't working three-fourths of the time.

The pictures we got were poor to say the least. (I'm enclosing an example.) So we're still trying to get a picture, but nothing so fanciful. Actually I think the choir idea will work much better when they're several years older. And better yet, Cleora, let's

At least Pat is singing.

take it sometime when you're here — we could use your choir-directing experience.

Today Bob came home at noon, we put them all in the car, and went over to the cemetery where we have uncluttered scenery with no house, and tried more pictures — but Eric absolutely wouldn't do anything right. I was making like a matador with my red coat, doing all kinds of things trying to entertain him, but all he'd do was look at the ground. I understand that one can buy lovely commercial Christmas cards at reasonable prices.

Bob is about ready to check into the church budget. Every Saturday night he studies and studies his lesson, then teaches his class Sunday morning. Usually at least two nights a month he's at a board meeting or some such thing, and occasionally does other things while I do very little at the church. Of course he receives no pay for his work.

Yesterday I helped in the nursery. Barbara Derby, a close neighbor, is in charge of it. She and I had eight children including Eric and her Mary, and miraculously they all behaved beautifully (usually have more children plus crying). So Barbara and I chatted for 1 1/2 hours while Bob struggled with both Mike and Steve upstairs. For this I was paid $1.50. Bob feels there's just no justice. (It is a bit ridiculous that I was paid, I must admit. I guess the WSCS takes care of the pay for child care.)

Mike just arrived home from a birthday party with a package of play money. He says he won it in a contest — I'm impressed. Steve has been playing at Mark's house so it's been quiet here. Eric as usual has been playing with pens. Carla is here playing with Pat. They usually get along beautifully now, and today was no exception.

Last night we put up our first Christmas decoration, the Santa mobile in the kitchen. Today I got out our Mahalia Jackson Christmas record, and it's beginning to feel like Christmas around here. Incidentally, I have a small package to mail toward the end of this week — this one we'd like you to open just as soon as you get it. It's your Christmas gift from the children, but we think you'll enjoy it more before Christmas than you would if you opened it on the 25th.

Mike has brought home his first reading book several times, and I'm so thrilled when he reads it to the other children. He simply can't remember the word "go," and asks us over and over. He got quite a blow, though, when he was reading, came to it, said, "What's that?" and Steve cheerfully answered, "Go." Mike looked shocked and seems to be able to remember the word now.

Eric had a gay evening the other night along with the rest of us. Bob decided to stay home from Barbershop practice because he was tired. Then he suddenly started making fudge, and popcorn, and cutting up apples. We had a feast. (Guess I hadn't fixed much supper.)

Just as we were starting to eat, Eric woke up, crying hard. We gave him drinks, patted his back, even gave him aspirin for he has a cold, but nothing calmed him down. So I brought him out in the living room. He calmed down and ate apples until he noticed the popcorn (which I thought he'd never had so didn't know enough to like it), and demanded some (and got it). I managed to keep the fudge out of his reach.

After he'd had a good snack, he jumped down, trotted off toward his bedroom. I opened the door, he went over to the bed, and tried to get in. When I lifted him up, he lay down very contentedly. Suppose he'll be the type of man always getting up in the middle of the night to eat?

Love, Jeanne

December 19, 1958

Dear Dad and Cleora,

Only six more days! We can hardly wait.

We've had a lovely week even though Eric was sick Monday and Tuesday. I wondered if I'd have to give up entirely the entertaining I had in mind. Tuesday I made two recipes of Christmas bread. I froze one poinsettia, then served it to the neighbors Thursday morning. The two "trees" and another poinsettia are in two friends' freezers. They think they're doing me a favor (which they definitely are) by storing my Christmas baking until Tuesday when I'll pick it up. Actually I'll visit each one Tuesday, take my package out of their freezers, wish them a Merry Christmas, and hand one to each of them.

The poinsettia goes to Roberta and Wayne Murphey, the ones who always give us the lovely box of homemade candy. Tuesday or Wednesday I'll make another batch of stollen, this one into four loaves, one for each next-door neighbor, one for Dr. and Mrs. Cooley, and one for our Christmas breakfast.

Did I ever tell you how much we liked the choirboy Christmas card you sent the children? Mike looked at all our cards hanging up on the wall, pointed to that one, and said, "That's my favorite."

Yesterday morning the pre-school children came an hour earlier than their mothers, and made cookies. We had a fine time. I'm planning the school-age baking party for Monday. Mike wants to have something – he feels he's missed quite a bit this week while he was at school. He had his school party this afternoon, and came home with a plastic "missile" which pleases him.

This morning four of the Theta Sigs and their children came over for coffee, stollen, and cookies. It was a little wilder than yesterday (eight children) because these children weren't used to playing together as the neighbor children are, but we had fun.

Eric is fine now. He had a very high fever Monday and Tuesday, perhaps the flu, although he never threw up. He just lay on the sectional most of the time, going to sleep frequently during the day, even with all the racket around here. He looked so pathetic. He took lots of baby aspirin, and seems all right now.

Eric was rather upset for a while this morning. About 20 minutes before the company came, he stuck his head in that wooden shoeshine bucket he plays with. He likes to put toys in it, and loves to carry it around. Anyhow, he got his head stuck!

I was down in the basement and heard him crying. When I got upstairs, Steve had pulled Eric's head out, but Eric was extremely indignant.

We're driving to Arthur Christmas morning to be with Bob's parents. Marge and her family will be there. Christmas should be exciting with seven kids aged one to six.

Love, Jeanne

PART III

1959
Final Year in Iowa

Christmas card photo, 1958

January 6, 1959

Dear Dad and Cleora,

Your Christmas package was wonderful. Mike put on his cowboy shirt the minute he opened his gift. He loves it and it looks fabulous on him. I had to have it washed and ironed for the first day of school yesterday. He's so proud.

Steve loves his tractor. I wish you could have seen his eyes when he opened his package. And Eric likes pull toys and enjoys his corn popper a lot. He also likes the little squeak toy. Sometimes he plays with it in the bathtub, sometimes out.

Pat's had a doll suitcase for a couple of years, but she liked it so much, it was about done for. I wanted to buy her one for her new doll clothes but decided not to. So I was about as pleased as she was when we saw the pretty diaper bag. She likes her new doll dress too. We're both enjoying her doll. She's just finished bathing it, and will probably be out soon for help with dressing it. New Year's Day we figured out how to make it cry real tears.

Christmas Eve we attended a candle-light service at a little Lutheran church near here, the only church in West Des Moines with an early service to which we could take our children. Not being used to church services, Eric, who always stays in the nursery at our church, was a pill. He was thrilled to death with the entire proceedings. When he's thrilled, he's awfully noisy about it.

I had put his pajamas on him, and apparently he'd assumed he'd be going to bed. The surprise of being taken out among all those people almost overwhelmed him. After about ten minutes of my trying to quiet him, and actually exciting him all the more, Bob took over. Poor Bob – he was almost a wreck when we got

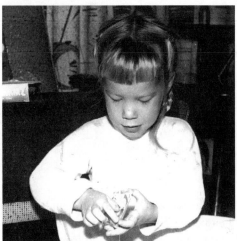

Pat – Christmas at Grandpa Lindsay's

home – but he and Eric looked so sweet in church!

On the way out, the young minister asked if we were new in town. I told him no, we were just Methodists, but we had no early service.

Christmas morning I think we broke some kind of precedent. We set our alarm for 5:30, got up, made our bed, got dressed, started breakfast, and had half our own presents opened before Mike woke up! He was shocked for he'd been telling us how he was going to wake up first and get all the rest of us up. Then he woke up the other children. They had opened a few gifts, mostly from each other, Christmas Eve, and they understood that Santa knew they'd be in Arthur Christmas morning.

Bob and I had a good breakfast – eggs, Christmas stollen, bacon, and toast. I even had time to clean up the kitchen while he got ready. At 7:30 we were on our way to Arthur, and it worked out beautifully. We hadn't had to hurry the children, and we hadn't asked them to eat breakfast with us. Instead, I cooked a package of wieners, some toast, and took some apples for them to eat in the car. It may sound like an odd breakfast, but they loved it. They'd had milk and orange juice at home.

We figured they'd be getting so much candy and trash in Arthur, we'd better get some food into them on the way. And that's certainly not a slam at Mother L.'s Christmas dinner. It was delicious. It's just that grandparents traditionally allow children more candy than parents do . . . and on Christmas Day we don't want to be strict.

Bob and I got our little transistor radio for ourselves for Christmas and we enjoyed that so much for the Christmas music on the trip. We'd never had a radio in our car before. Christmas afternoon Bob gave me a heavy dog collar chain with padlock which mystified the relatives. He got it so he could chain our radio into his little car during the day because he can't lock the car.

Marge's three kids and our four behaved pretty well Christmas Day. There were four extra relatives, making 17 of us. Pat managed to create something of a scene by falling off her chair during dinner, which I maintain couldn't possibly be an accident. She's a shrill-voiced little thing right now and loves to scream. We're rather strenuously encouraging her to forget the screaming. Think we'll have any luck?

Friday evening Dick and Marge took their children over to a neighbor in Arthur, where a cow would be milked. At first we were going to take our children too. We'd never thought of it before, but they'd never seen a cow milked. However, we decided seven children would be just too much for the poor cow.

Marge and Dick took Mike along with them. The woman even let him try milking the cow. He was thrilled. Has Dad told you, Cleora, that Mike has said for a long time that he's not going to get married? Instead, he's going to live with Grandpa Warren when he grows up. He'd love to spend some time on the farm if you ever want him.

Marge and Dick left early Saturday morning. Eric had vomited Christmas night, but we figured he ate too much plus the excitement. However, apparently he had 24-hour flu. Saturday morning Steve was sick, felt rotten all day. That afternoon Pat got it and Bob was feeling queasy. But at 5:45 we started home because we wanted to be here Sunday morning for the dedication of our new church, and also for Bob's Sunday School class.

Bob says he felt fairly well most of the way home. He drove, and made it into our driveway, but was violently sick the minute he stepped out of the car. I managed to get the car unpacked and the kids dumped into bed before it hit me. Mike was sick in the night, and Bob and I took turns getting up with him. We couldn't help him much because each one of us had to run to the bathroom constantly. Mike apparently understood the situation and didn't feel mistreated as we left him in his top bunk with a pan. It really wasn't as grim as it all sounds. It lasted such a short time.

Sunday we mostly lay around, except Eric, who was feeling

Christmas in Arthur – Brad, Curt, Steve, Eric, Mike, Pat, Amy

wonderful. He's such a neat little soul that he persisted in picking up things and trying to put them away or give them to us.
You can imagine the mess we were in. By Sunday evening we
were okay. We haven't even had colds during the past month, so
actually have had better-than-usual health which is wonderful,
especially at Christmastime.

New Year's Eve we went to a movie, then to a friend's home
for their Open House. New Year's Day Bob slept until time for
the Rose Bowl Parade while Pat and I played with her doll. At
noon we fixed cheese and ham sandwiches. Our minister, Dr.
Cooley, and his wife had invited us out for dinner. We went to
a restaurant for shrimp, then to their home to talk fishing for
a couple of hours. He sent home with us four of the fish he'd
caught in Minnesota last summer. Mrs. Cooley was tired of
having them in her freezer.

We've had the Cooleys over for dinner a few times, and they
kept talking about repaying us. As we told them, this was ridiculous. Both Bob and I grew up to think that if you wanted to, you
had your minister and his family over for dinner occasionally,
with no thought of going to their house in return. We find that a

big church isn't nearly that friendly. Dr. and Mrs. Cooley actually appear to be a little lonely. When we took them some stollen Christmas Eve, they seemed shocked.

Saturday night Roberta and Wayne Murphey and their 11-year-old son, Bobbie, visited us. Bob had a wonderful time helping Bobbie build an elaborate cabin with Mike's new American log set. Incidentally, both Bob and I have had a great time playing with those logs, and also with Steve's hardwood train and track set. (The boys like them too.)

Going tobogganing with the youth group Sunday night was fun. I loved whizzing down the big hills at the park in Des Moines. Going up was a different matter. I discovered I couldn't keep up with the kids! What a blow. Especially when this cute little eighth grader started treating me in such a solicitous manner, more or less the way I was taught to treat my great aunt Belle. I'm sure he meant well, but I told Bob I know now how his father feels.

It worries Bob and his mother because Dad can't do quite as many things as he used to do, but still keeps trying. That was my trouble Sunday night. Bob sat out a ride or two at first, but I persisted in going with them every time, until I had to quit. It was fun, and I'm not *very* stiff today.

Steve got a tool set for Christmas. The other day we stopped in a lumber yard and got a box of scrap lumber. He's making the sawdust fly downstairs. His saw is wicked looking. I hope all our chairs can keep their legs.

I've mentioned before how Pat detested the empire dress I made her last fall. I made a matching one for her doll, and gave Pat a pair of red leotard stockings for Christmas. She was quite happy with matching her dolly Christmas day, and apparently doesn't mind her dress now. I tell her it's the only one that her stockings go with. She looks cute, but long stockings, even red ones, look strange after seeing her in anklets all these years.

After thoroughly disliking long stockings when I was little because I had to wear them more than my friends, it's hard to get used to seeing Pat in them.

Love, Jeanne

February 5, 1959

Dear Dad and Cleora,

I'm trying to remember yesterday so I can think about it on the day Steve receives his diploma from medical school. The doll pills fascinated him, and one poor doll with a mouth just open enough to stuff a pill inside must be stock full of the things.

He can't quite understand the purpose of the microscope, but he's sure it's good for something. He's checked all our eyes, taken his bear's and each doll's temperature, and treats Pat when she lets him. He was very serious as he checked her heart last night. When Bob came home, he (Bob) carefully listened to each child's heart. He says the stethoscope really works.

This morning Steve and Eric got dressed for the first time since the red measles started. Eric isn't well yet, but he won't stay in bed, so might as well be dressed. Besides, he trotted over to the ironing, picked up his coveralls, and brought them to me with the most pleased expression this morning. I couldn't resist him.

Steve is much better. He doesn't look red at all in comparison with the others. Pat seems a little worse today, but I'm sure it's because I'm finally paying more attention to her. She slept all day long Monday, and stayed down part of Tuesday and Wednesday. During these three days, Eric took all the attention he could get. Today he's finally started playing.

Eric is the most atrocious looking little thing you can imagine – they were all very red, but perhaps because he's little, he's the reddest one. He looks pretty pathetic. Yesterday afternoon he cried a good share of the time. I tried to hold him, rock him, lie down with him, but the only thing he wanted was for me to carry him and walk the floor. I can't do that with a 20-month-old. Eric also is throwing things, violently. I think he'll do better next week when he's feeling good.

You reacted quickly after you received the card I wrote Monday morning. We received the box Wednesday at breakfast and loved it. I liked all the desk supplies (tacks, tape, glue, etc.), and everything else, too. Steve and Pat haven't been eating much. (Mike didn't either when he had the measles.) With candy cigarettes for dessert, it was amazing how their appetites perked up.

Mike has been making Valentines every day this week. Most of them seem to be for girls. He brought home a very pretty one from a little girl named Nancy Paul, and spent the most time making hers.

This morning I came out of Steve's room to find Eric gleefully scattering the powder from a new can of talcum all over the sectional and rug. Pat was lying on the other sectional, quietly watching him. I asked her later why she didn't call me when she saw him doing it. "Oh, I just laughed to him," she answered.

Today I opened the draperies and shades for the first time this week and it's wonderful. This constant twilight because of the measles was getting me down. I like lots of light. But the three small ones didn't seem to have as much eye trouble as Mike did. He watched TV for the first couple of days, then finally went to a dark room for several days. For the others, we started out with rather strenuously dim rooms and no TV. Apparently it was the way to go.

Pat just got dressed and seems to feel 100 percent better. Combing her hair to get it out of her eyes probably helped as much as anything, even though she didn't want me to do it.

I just made some instant chocolate pudding. I tried to make it special by folding miniature marshmallows into it. Then I remembered a recipe that also added peppermint flavoring, so I dumped some in. When I tasted it, I realized it apparently takes very little. It tastes awfully minty, and I have a sneaking suspicion my children won't appreciate it.

Love, Jeanne

February 12, 1959

Dear Dad and Cleora,

Mike is sitting here working on Valentines again. As he was furiously writing, he looked up to say, "I really hate her, but I'm saying I like her."

He finished writing, looked at it, then said in a shocked voice, "I said I loved her!" And he immediately started erasing.

"Why are you erasing it?" I asked.

"Because I don't," he responded.

Eric is smiling again. Bob commented on it last night. There were a few days last week when we were afraid he'd forgotten how. He still has red cheeks, but otherwise is over the measles. So are Pat and Steve. Steve, however, whose red spots left first, about five days ago, has a bad cold now and spent this morning lying down – against his wishes, naturally.

Pat, Steve, and Eric are looking better now. All looked pretty awful. Pat, no matter how carefully I combed her hair and put a nice dress on her, simply didn't look attractive at all with the measles. Eric looked outlandishly silly, or pathetic, whichever you choose.

This afternoon I decided I definitely do not like having two cars. Ice covered everything here Sunday and Monday morning. Then we got quite a lot of snow that drifted badly, mainly into our driveway. The red station wagon was parked nearly to the end of the driveway, and I haven't been out since Friday afternoon. This Friday afternoon I plan to attend a League of Women Voters meeting downtown, so today I went out to shovel snow after lunch.

Bob parked the little blue TR2 out beyond the sidewalk last

night because of the snow, and casually suggested it would be nice if I got some shoveling done today. Normally I wouldn't bother unless the kids could go out with me. But Bob has had a horribly bad chest cough and cold for nearly four weeks now. The doctor is treating him for his asthma too, and he just hasn't gotten well yet. Anyhow, I went out to shovel, and decided I'd better go clear up to the back of the red car. It took nearly 45 minutes of the hardest shoveling I've ever done to get it cleared out. I left the 2-4 inches of ice on the driveway.

Pat and Eric were in bed, but I let Steve stay up and watch me. He "baby-sat." He was to call me if the phone rang or Pat or Eric needed something. Steve came to the door once to ask me please to jump in the deep snow. He'll be happy when he can go back out to play. I was pretty stiff when I came in. I guess Bob's right when he says I don't get much exercise.

As for Bob's cough – every morning I attempt to talk him into staying home, but he doesn't think he needs to. His worst day was the Monday that Steve, Pat and Eric felt the worst from the measles. Bob said he told the people at work he'd go home except he had three sick kids at home and doubted that he'd get any sympathy.

Love, Jeanne

Steve and Pat – Valentine photos for Grandpa and Grandma.

February 16, 1959

Dear Dad and Cleora,

I keep losing my voice, which is frustrating but much more pleasant than feeling ill. At breakfast today I couldn't make a sound above a whisper. Bob said to the children, "Now you listen to Mommy today. Her voice is bad and she can't talk, so when she whispers, you pay attention – she might be yelling at you!"

This past month I've not had any sewing to do, didn't want to clean or do anything else really useful. So I've been clipping, pasting, and filing the recipes I've been saving for several years. Naturally I can't resist trying some of them. Bob and the kids are about to mutiny in favor of hamburgers and fried potatoes.

Tonight I'm trying a new recipe for spaghetti in which you simmer the sauce for an hour, then add a cup of red wine, and simmer for another hour. "All the alcoholic content will cook away, leaving only the wonderful flavor," said the recipe. But the whole house smelled like a wine factory as the sauce cooked, and I don't much like the smell or taste of wine. The spaghetti will be interesting, I'm sure.

When Bob saw the groceries I bought Saturday for the next two weeks, he shuddered. I had Swiss, Parmesan, and cheddar cheese, and different kinds of cheese usually means I'll be trying different recipes. Bob likes his cheese not sharp, and simply served with raw apples, not cooked. Next week I'm trying a casserole of hamburger, cottage cheese, Swiss cheese, and noodles.

This afternoon I'm going to a tea at the Art Center. The membership drive is starting and I'm helping with it. I had sitter trouble, so finally asked Barbara Derby if the three young ones could stay with her. She needed a bed for Eric. This morning,

Pat does very well with her hula hoop.

rather than lift it into the car, I folded his crib and wheeled it up the sidewalk to her house. Luckily the ice is frozen hard. In the process, one corner of the 30-year-old crib pulled apart. I hope it recovers.

Pat loves her hula hoop. On these cold stormy days, it's good she has something she enjoys doing in the basement.

February 18. Mike is home today. The teachers are visiting other schools "to gain new ideas in the teaching field," according to the note he brought home.

The tea at the art center was nice, but I don't think I'll go again. Instead of giving us our envelopes and instructions, then letting us depart in peace, they served coffee and doughnuts (and me on a diet). Then we all milled around for ages, then finally went into the meeting room. There we heard a long talk by the Art Center director, and then the membership drive chairman chattered for a while. Mostly, she read word for word the instructions on our envelopes. One would think they'd get literate people to help so they wouldn't feel they must read the directions to everyone.

Love, Jeanne

March 13, 1959

Dear Dad and Cleora,

We've had a lovely blizzard, the worst – or the best – since I've lived in Iowa. Bob made it home last night, and he was luckier than some. He left the TR at Solar. He knew he couldn't get home in it because the drifts were higher than the car is. Bob got a ride to within three blocks of home. Walking into the 30-mile wind and snow with nothing on his head and no boots or overshoes wasn't much fun. His asthma kicked in, and he was a mess when he got home.

This morning he left confidently at 7:30 (dressed for the weather this time) in the Plymouth, and got all of two blocks away from home. He came back about 10:30 after having bought chains for the Plymouth. He and Mike walked up to put them on the car after lunch, and he's out now, maybe at work although I'm not sure.

A blizzard is kind of cozy if you get home. Both Nadean and Bob next door were without cars. Nadean got stuck three blocks from here last night, and Bob left his car up on Ashworth. So they came over for coffee about 11 a.m. after he shoveled out his driveway. They're selling their house and moving back to Beaverdale which we regret.

This week I made a silly white blouse for the blue suit I made last year. I never did like the suit, but thought a white blouse with the jacket worn open might help. It's a short overblouse, hanging straight to about an inch below my waist. A couple of weeks ago we went shopping and actually got several things on sale – a blue poplin car coat for me and material for a plaid shirtwaist spring and summer dress, plus a cotton knit top with elastic around the

Pat helps Eric with his mittens so they can play in the snow.

bottom for which I must make tan pants.

Last night while the blizzard was still raging, a friend phoned to invite us to a tobogganing party Saturday night. We'll meet at Waveland Park, and then go to our friends' home afterward to dance. Sounds like fun. I think I told you about the tobogganing party with the church MYF group in January, and that I couldn't keep up with the kids. I'm expecting this party to consist of other people as old and worn down as we are!

Love, Jeanne

May 20, 1959

Dear Dad and Cleora,

An entire week without the children. Pure joy! We left them with Bob's parents, and drove to Colorado two weeks ago Saturday.

Sunday we saw the sports car races in La Junta. They were interesting, but watching one goes a long way. We're not too eager to see races often. Sunday night we drove over to Cañon City, visited the Royal Gorge that night and the next morning, then had the most beautiful back-road drive over to Pike's Peak. It was a mountain road, unpaved, with nobody on it but a couple of road maintenance groups. Apparently the road had just been opened.

We had a wonderful vacation. We didn't have to put the top on the Triumph at all, although it snowed, rained and sleeted on us on Pike's Peak. As we started up, it was snowing and raining, and the man said we'd better put the top up. He didn't real-ize what a job that is, and that we had no intention of doing so. Instead we got out the big plastic sheet we'd bought for just such an emergency, and put it over us. Each of us held one corner up over the windshield. The cars coming down probably thought they were meeting a maniac and should take for the hills (in this case, the mountain).

Soon we stopped for lunch and the weather cleared. This was our second day in Colorado, and I hadn't learned how to dress warmly yet, so we weren't very comfortable at the top in all the snow. We stood around the little stove in the lodge for a while. Then when we went out to see the view, a fog rolled in so we drove back down. Soon it started to sleet, but we didn't mind that because it wasn't wet.

That night we drove on to Denver and stayed with friends that night and the next day. Tuesday was more or less wasted in downtown Denver. The car brakes were grabbing a little, and this isn't too comforting on mountain roads, so we had them repaired.

The odometer had also gone out the night before, so we had that fixed, and had the car greased. We bought cowboy boots for the boys ($5 each at a surplus store).

Wayne Ventling, who works with Bob at Solar, invited us to stay in his cabin west of Denver. I had never met Wayne before, and we had no idea what to expect, but decided to spend two nights in the cabin. After we saw it, we wished we'd spent the entire week there. We were completely alone, high up on a mountain with a rushing stream right behind us. The house was decorated just right for a vacation house, with an old-fashioned black pot-bellied stove which put out lots of heat about two minutes after Bob lit it. I wanted to stay there for at least a day and do nothing, but we didn't take the time. We wanted to see Estes Park.

Jeanne – It's a trifle chilly out here.

On the way home Friday we stopped in Sterling, Colorado, and Bob had his three-week-old beard shaved to an Abe Lincoln look with a mustache.

The kids had a great time with Mother and Dad Lindsay. The other day Mike and Steve asked me why they couldn't live with Grandma and Grandpa – and they weren't even mad at me at the time. We thought Eric would be thrilled to see us. But when he came downstairs Saturday morning and saw us in the bed in the living room, he mostly ignored us. In fact, he hid behind Grandma's skirt. Then he walked into her room and had her dress him, then condescended to come out to see us. He grew up a lot while we were gone, and has the run of the neighborhood now. He even learned a few words that week.

Oh yes, Bob's beard – I wish you could have seen him. He shaved it off Saturday, much to my disappointment. He looked absolutely wonderful with it, a little older, but more handsome too. Now he looks ridiculously young, comparatively. He got tired of all the attention it got him. I can't understand why people couldn't treat it as just something he liked instead of constantly asking him why he did it, calling him Grandpa, telling him Beatnik jokes, etc. His boss didn't like it at all which I think is completely ridiculous. I took several pictures of him before he shaved it off.

Colorado is celebrating its Centennial this year, which was Bob's excuse for not shaving during the three weeks of his vacation. Then we liked the beard so he kept it, until now. Our minister didn't appreciate the beard either. He obviously didn't like the idea of having a bearded chairman of the board.

Love, Jeanne

June 22, 1959

Dear Dad and Cleora,

Mike is in the hospital.

Friday morning we went over to the wading pool and had a wonderful time. All four kids loved the water. Eric went under once and came up sputtering. I dashed in, fished him out, and dried his face, thinking he must be terrified. But he immediately went back into the pool, giggling!

When we got home, I put Mike, Steve, and Pat in the shower. I asked Mike to turn off the shower, which he did. Suddenly he started screaming. He'd slipped, and cut his eyelid on the middle faucet.

I gave him a towel to put over it (dirty one, I'm afraid, although apparently it caused no extra trouble), got a pair of pants on him, and walked him up to Barbara, my RN neighbor four houses away. (I'm a little squeamish about examining this sort of thing, but have vowed not to be that way again.) She glanced at his eye, told me to bring the other kids up to her house (it was then 11:45 a.m.), and take Mike to the doctor.

The doctor, bless his heart, was in his office, but he looked at Mike and told me to take him to an oculist.

This of course meant going clear downtown, and me in dirty shorts and old, only-to-be-worn-in-an-ironing-emergency blouse. I called Bob but he was at lunch, and it would have been crazy for him to come after Mike anyhow. We finally found a parking place downtown two blocks from the oculist. Not a single policeman in sight to ask the nearest parking to Sixth and Locust. The cops miraculously appeared after we parked.

The oculist was in, looked at Mike, and said he'd *fix him

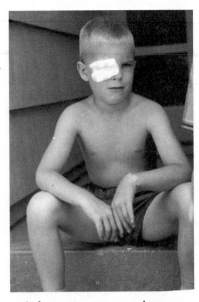

At least no permanent damage.

up" after office hours. He said Mike had to go over to Blank Hospital. I still thought this was just a simple stitching job, and that he'd be home that night with a patch over his eye. Dr. Lambrecht, the oculist, assured me there was no damage to Mike's eye, just the eyelid. He said a little hunk was completely gone which he'd look for when he worked on Mike. He also mentioned a slit clear through sideways.

We checked in at the hospital, and I learned Mike would be there overnight. At 4 p.m. Bob came over, and the doctor took Mike to surgery. They were in there until 6 p.m. (the longest two hours we'd had in a long time). Dr. Lambrecht came out assuring us he'd done a beautiful job. He went into great detail about his sewing methods, sounding, as Bob said, more expensive with every sentence. Don't misunderstand me – we're grateful we got a capable doctor, and it's wonderful that apparently Mike will have scarcely a scar. The doctor found the little missing piece of eyelid and sewed it back in.

When Mike came out of surgery, they told us we might as well not come back until 8 because he certainly wouldn't wake up before then. When we came back, Mike was asleep. He'd vomited a little. They didn't let him eat lunch, but before I knew that, I'd gotten him an ice cream bar to eat between the doctor and oculist's offices. We stayed around until nearly 10 p.m., but Mike still didn't awaken. We finally went home, and returned at 10 a.m. the next morning, when visiting hours began. He wasn't feeling well at all, and we learned that while he loved having one of us there, it was a little silly for both of us to stand around, so I came home, and we took turns from then on.

Yesterday he was feeling better, but as usual, doesn't eat

Eric plays Nadean's piano.

unless someone insists. He didn't want to sit up or get up if he could avoid it. We're explaining that we want him home (and he says he wants to come home), and that as long as he acts sick, he'll have to stay here.

I'm going to try to be there for lunch and supper as long as he's there to get him to eat. Sounds peculiar, I know, to insist that an ill child eat, but knowing Mike, I'm afraid it's necessary. Once last year he was sick, and obviously shouldn't eat, so we let him alone. After several days of this, he was so weak he really didn't want to eat. Somewhere along the line he's missed learning that it's fun to eat. With me as an example, you'd assume he would think differently.

I'd planned to take Steve, Pat, and Eric to the doctor 9-11 a.m. today. The sitter can't come until after swimming lessons, so I can't visit Mike until after 11. But the doctor isn't in, so I have an hour and a half to kill. I certainly don't want to spend it doing useful things like cleaning up the place. Pat and Steve are playing outside, and Eric and I are going over to Nadean's for a cup of coffee. Eric likes to play Nadean's piano.

Pat has had a stomachache almost every afternoon for a week, and yesterday we decided we should take her to the doctor. Steve and Eric each need an annual checkup and a shot of some kind, so I thought I'd get it all done at once. Pat's fine this morning, so it's probably just as well we're not going.

We've decided to go to Manhattan to see Betty and Carl over the Fourth. It's high time they meet Eric. We'll go down Thursday evening, and come home Sunday.

Love, Jeanne

July 20, 1959

Dear Dad and Cleora,

Mike had his stitches removed (under anesthetic) almost two weeks ago. You were right – he was quite disappointed because he can't even see his scar.

Remember the "poison ivy" I mentioned after our trip to Colorado? You suggested I'd better cure it or it would spread, and I said so brightly that it wasn't spreading. It's not poison ivy; it's a fungus according to our doctor. This sounds perfectly awful I think, but he tells me it's not my fault – it just happens.

It's spread a lot and I'm having a terrible time getting rid of it. Twice a day I soak my feet and hands in a bright purple solution, which stains them thoroughly. I'm sure every child on the block has come up and said, "Why are your hands and feet so dirty?" Some day I must think of a good answer.

Last week we had a friend's three boys, aged 4, 8, and 9, for two days. We're hoping to take Mike to Bob's sister near Chicago August 8 to spend a week. We want to go into Chicago ourselves and leave the other three at home. I thought this friend and I could trade some baby-sitting, for we know no sitters that will stay overnight even if we do want to pay that much. But I was quite disillusioned to find how much easier it is to care for older children. Our three young ones would give her fits, while her three took care of themselves while they were here. I'm still thinking maybe she can keep them overnight, and we'll have a young girl down the street (35¢ an hour) take care of them during the days. We might not even go, but I'd like to

Are you doing a lot of gardening, canning, and/or freezing? Our six tomato plants are just sitting still, not completely

Sunset Park Zoo – Howard W., Carl, and Bob with the Wood and Lindsay kids.

dying, but not growing at all. Our garden is a marsh this year, and we shouldn't have even tried tomatoes. I guess we should have planted rice instead, but we prefer the minute kind.

Bob and I have been wanting matching shirts but couldn't afford the $5 each for the ones we liked. We liked the new sport shirt I made Mike for church this summer so much that I got the same fabric this week for us. I finished Bob's, and hope to make mine this week.

We had a lovely trip to Manhattan – mostly. During the first five minutes of the trip, Eric, sitting in my lap in the front seat, threw up, Pat in the middle seat threw up, and

Pat liked sitting on Aunt Betty's lap.

Mike in the back seat also vomited, more or less simultaneously. Also, we had a flat tire after we had all the children laid out in the back of the car and almost asleep. Of course the spare tire was beneath them all! When we got to Betty's, we were fine.

Betty entertained us royally. Several college friends with all their children came over. One night it was Mary Ann and Herman Cott and their two sons plus Evelyn and Dallas Nelson and their two. The next night Peggy and Howard Wood came with their four daughters. Howard, Bob and Carl took all eight children to the Sunset Park Zoo while Peg, Betty, and I talked. Nice!

Love, Jeanne

August 20, 1959

Dear Dad and Cleora,

Last week Solar announced it's closing the Des Moines plant October 31 – such a way to celebrate Holloween! Bob is working on applications to various companies, some here in the Midwest, and some on the west coast. The aircraft industry is at its biggest on the west coast, and he also thinks we'd like living there.

Of course we'll sell our house. I'd hoped we could sell it "as is." However, Dr. and Mrs. Cooley came over for dinner the other night. When we told them our plans, Dr. Cooley looked at the walls in the living room, and commented, not especially tactfully, that we'd better paint all the rooms if we want to get a decent price for the house. So that's our plan in the next few weeks. I'd rather not bother.

Steve starts kindergarten next week. He's extremely excited. He's been eager to go ever since Mike started two years ago. I wonder if he'll insist on wearing Bob's Boy Scout cap the first day.

Have you heard of a White Elephant sale among friends? Our block tried it last week. Each of us took things, mostly children's clothes, that we didn't want, put a price tag on them, hung them on a neighbor's clothesline or laid them on the picnic table, then at 3 p.m. we each bought what we wanted. I didn't sell much of anything, but bought a petticoat for Pat for 35¢, boots for Eric for 25¢, a new nylon topper suit for him for $1, robe for Mike for 50¢, white shirt for Steve (too small for him really) for 10¢, and a white hooded sweatshirt for Eric for 50¢.

Our lives are going to change a lot when we move. There is one bright spot, however. Somehow I managed to end up finance chairman for PTA this fall. No one else would do it, and they assured me I wouldn't have to do much. So I went to the first committee meeting last week. The other women there were all excited about raising money by throwing a carnival at school.

They chattered on about their plans for awhile, then suddenly someone turned to me and said, "You're chairman. How do you feel about having a carnival?"

I responded as cheerfully as possible, but did mention that I didn't much like carnivals. The conversation continued, and we're having a carnival in October. If I'm lucky, we will have moved by then . . .

I've enjoyed this house and this neighborhood, but moving sounds pretty exciting. I wonder where we'll be living . . .

A couple of nights ago we got a lot of rain. Eric went out to play the next morning. Apparently he rolled in the mud! I suspect he got some help from Pat and Carla.

Love, Jeanne

Such a forlorn looking little creature.

October 14, 1959

Dear Dad and Cleora,

I'm sitting here in the mood that if I ever chewed my fingernails, I'd probably do that right now. Since I don't have that outlet, can't get interested in magazines, and don't dare make the slightest mess around here, I decided to write to you. The reason I'm a little twitchy right now is that so many things are happening all at once that I'm not quite sure what's going on.

We've had an interesting couple of months with all these applications. It's been quite a process. Job application forms tend to be the most complicated pieces of paper I've helped fill out for a while. Each time Bob brings a new one home, I read the literature and get all excited about that particular area. Phoenix has the best Chamber of Commerce, we thought, for their spiel on weather and living conditions was fabulous. Cedar Rapids sounds good to me, and so does California.

The painting is done, and the house looks lovely. It is now for sale, and I'm trying hard to keep *everything* picked up so it will look good if anyone comes to see it. I try not even to leave my coffee cup in the sink. I'm also trying not to be too crabby with the kids when they leave stuff out. It will be nice when this part is over.

All morning a neighbor and I wrapped candy for the PTA carnival which is to be at school Friday night. At 11:30 a realtor called, asking if she could show our house between 1 and 2 p.m., which is why I can't do something sensible like sleep right now.

I phoned Bob to verify that we wanted her to ask $15,000 (we've been asking $14,500), which would net us about $14,100 minus selling costs. Her commission would be 6 percent. Bob, bless his heart, called the realtor and told her that we hadn't signed anything, and that we had to have at least that much clear. If she wanted to ask less, and get less commission, that was fine.

I don't often pull a helpless female act like this, but when Bob suggested I call her back with all this, and I wasn't thrilled with the idea, he agreed to do it himself. He's leaving the advertising and showing the house up to me. But when we start talking terms, he's willing to be involved, and that's where I need help.

At noon another woman called and said she was quite interested. When I told her when we might leave, she said they'd be out this evening.

Monday night a couple was here and seemed *very* interested, the first real interest anyone had shown. But they didn't have the $2900 down payment, only $1100. He was going to try to borrow the rest, and we haven't heard from them again. We had an attorney over last night explaining how to sell on a real estate contract, so we're ready for that too.

Pat loves the pajamas you sent her for her birthday. She's worn them every night since she got them. She'll be quite upset the first bad day when I wash them and can't get them dry by bedtime. She's enjoyed her doll so much too. Did you notice how she pronounced "ballerina" on the phone to you that morning? She had a little trouble, but got out a reasonable facsimile of it.

We took Mike to the doctor Friday evening and Saturday noon. His ear was in rather bad shape. They gave him a shot and sent him home with a bottle of antibiotics ($4.50 per half-bottle), which cleared it all up. He went back to school yesterday.

I can't seem to get my cold cleared up, but it's lots better. So far Bob hasn't had even the sniffles, and of course he's most eager not to get sick at this point. In fact, he hasn't kissed me properly in the three weeks since my cold started. This morning he had a slight sore throat, and is taking a thermos of orange juice to work with him, his favorite cure.

An added complication today – it's Carla's birthday and Pat is to go there after her nap and stay for supper. Mike has a 3:45 dental appointment, so Eric and I will meet the boys at school and go to that appointment. If Pat isn't awake by then, Marcia (Carla's first grade sister) will stop here on her way home from school and wait for Pat. Steve, Pat and I went to the dentist yesterday, and Bob did last week. Bob had one filling, mine were cleaned, and that's all. We should get by economically this time. So far, none of the children has had a cavity.

Ray Norton of Waste King in Los Angeles called Bob about a job. At Norton's request, Bob flew to Chicago yesterday (left here at 5 a.m., was back at Solar at 2 p.m.) to be psychoanalyzed for Waste King – which I'm afraid I took rather lightly and thought amusing. He must have done all right because Norton asked him when he could fly out there at Waste King's expense to see them. Bob said this Friday, so he's leaving tomorrow for LA. He hopes he can leave tomorrow night, because tonight the man from Aerojet in Sacramento is coming in. Bob will take him out to dinner tonight, and he (the Aerojet man) will interview three other production control men at Solar tomorrow. Bob doesn't want to leave before the Aerojet rep does.

The Aerojet job might mean that Bob would go out to start

something new in production control for them, with three or four other Solar men going with him to work for him.

When Bob went in to tell his boss about leaving again tomorrow, Bob suggested that Jim might prefer to

The Triumph needed washing so Mike and Pat pitch in. lay him off tomorrow. Jim seemed interested in the idea and said he would let him know this afternoon. So, this means Bob might be working in California starting November 1. If this happens, we – or just Bob, if the house isn't sold (horrible thought) – would leave within a week or ten days.

I think he'll stay in LA until Sunday or Monday. Dr. Cooley is out there this week on some sort of a deal whereby he'll preach in an LA church this Sunday and Bob would love to attend. Also, if Bob takes the job, he'll probably want time to find a place for us to live. He'll stay with Hamlins while he's there.

Last weekend Bob and the children took time out to wash the TR-2. It was an enthusiastic laundry event.

Something else to figure out now, but very minor, is a way to get Mike and Steve, and possibly Pat, to the school carnival Friday night without Bob. I had thought I'd get a sitter for Pat and Eric and take Steve and Mike. Thank goodness, I'm not signed up to do anything special that night. (I told the ladies I couldn't be counted on because I might be gone by carnival time.) But Pat might feel bad if I leave her home. And now I'm wondering if Paula might, for her regular fee or slightly higher, just go with me, and we'd take all four. It might even be worth the 35¢ to get someone else to stay with Eric, and Paula and I would keep the other three happy. Mike's been looking forward to it for quite a while.

My biggest worry about leaving here next week is, will the children miss out on Trick or Treat night? I think they anticipate Halloween most next to Christmas and their birthdays. But we're likely to be here yet. If not, and we are in L.A., they could go out with the Hamlin children. The eight of them (Hamlins' youngest is probably too small to trick or treat) would make quite a dent in people's treats, wouldn't they?

So now I'm not nervous anymore! I do hope the house sells soon though.

Love, Jeanne

November 12, 1959

Dear Dad and Cleora,

It's finally happening, and fast. As you know, Bob decided on the job at Waste King in Los Angeles. Two weeks ago he drove both cars out, rather, drove the station wagon and towed the TR behind it. He and Woody Spears, who went with him on his way to a new job in San Diego, stopped in Fullerton. Nadean Phillips, who used to live next door, had told her father and his wife Bob was coming, and they said he could park the Triumph there until he finds a place to live. Well, he and Woody ended up spending the weekend with Paul and Mabel Johnson. Very nice.

We agreed that the children and I would come out to California to live by the middle of December even if the house hadn't sold, much as we didn't like the idea of leaving it empty. Well, wonder of wonders, it sold last Sunday. And now I can leave my coffee cup in the sink. Such a relief.

Dr. Cooley dropped by a couple of days ago. He says he doesn't want us to live in Hollywood (no intention of doing that), but he thinks some suburban areas might be acceptable "since we're young and enthusiastic." I think he's been a bit bothered by all this. Bob was the church chairman of the board, you know.

While Dr. Cooley and I were sitting in the living room talking, Steve sauntered in, came over to me and asked, "Why don't we ever say a blesing anymore?"

"Well . . . did we miss today? We were kind of busy, weren't we?" I asnwered, trying to shoo him away gently.

"But we didn't yesterday either."

And Dr. Cooley sat there and roared!

Incidentally, Steve said the blessing tonight.

The children seem to be handling all this pretty well. I've tried to explain exactly what's going on, and at this point, they seem excited too. Knowing their friends, the Hamlin children, will be there helps, and of course they're eager to be with Daddy. We've all missed him so much.

A job well done, Steve.

The packers are coming Monday, and the children and I are leaving next Tuesday. We'll fly into Kansas City, and stay with you until Friday evening, when we'll take a jet out of KC to Los Angeles.

We're delighted that Betty and Carl will probably be in Garnett at least part of the time we're there.

We had a lot of snow today, and the children had a wonderful time playing in it. I took pictures so I can show them after we move. I don't want them to forget what snow is like. As you know, I've never been out of the Midwest, and I can't imagine what it'll be like not to have a real winter. Carol Hamlin has written me about the parkas we won't need, the jeans the boys will wear to school as they do here, etc.

We plan to live in Orange County, or at least in that general area. The children are thrilled that we may be very close to Disneyland.

I suppose this week's snow storm is about the children's last. No more building igloos or snowmen . . . but we can go to the mountains when we're hungry for snow.

With Daddy gone, Steve decided to shovel off the sidewalk. He is deeply appreciated.

Love, Jeanne

November 29, 1959

Dear Dad and Cleora,

Thank you for taking such good care of us while we were with you. We had a crisis at the airport. Steve lost his teddy bear. He was quite upset, and I was thinking what a terrible way to start his first plane trip. But Carl saved the day. He found the bear in the men's room, and all was well.

Mike, Steve, and Pat sat in front of me on the plane, while Eric and I sat by a man from LA. The children behaved well, except for the few minutes Mike, Steve, and Pat were fighting over one blanket. Each one grabbed a corner, stood up, and they all pulled as hard as they could. The stewardess managed to find two more blankets, so that crisis, too, was solved.

We were all thrilled to see Bob at the airport. We went immediately to Hamlins in Canoga Park where we stayed all week. Saturday Bob and I left the children with Carol and Max while we went house hunting in Buena Park. We found a four-bedroom, two-bath house with a *tiny* back yard that we could afford, so we rented it.

Thanksgiving was nice at the Hamlins. Only hard part was that Carol and I each have always depended on someone else to make the gravy. We did our best, but it looked pretty anemic. So Carol grabbed some food coloring and mixed in a little red and a little green, until it looked nicely brown.

The truck finally came the day after Thanksgiving, and we're moving in. I'll take Mike and Steve to the nearby school and get them started Monday.

Our new life has begun!

Love, Jeanne

PART IV

1963 Postscript
Our Bonus Baby

The whole family including Paul and Mabel Johnson celebrate Erin's christening. Back row: Bob, Jeanne, Mabel, Paul; front: Steve, Mike, Pat, Erin, Eric

Introduction

The lives of the four little Lindsays and their parents changed in late 1959. We moved to California, bought a house in the almost new suburb of Buena Park in Orange County, and became part of the great Midwestern migration to the land of sunshine.

I went back to college to earn a teaching credential "for insurance." At that time, in my mind, Mom was still supposed to be home with the kids. I was rational enough, however, to realize life is not entirely certain, and I'd better have a better way of supporting four kids than counting on any chance to be the Brenda Starr of the newspaper world.

In 1963, I was almost ready to student teach. That fall, Eric would start kindergarten. I would be free at last for a few hours a day.

Something happened. The birth control pill was new and I wasn't on it yet. My diaphragm must have been in the dresser drawer again. I was pregnant.

When I told Bob, he made perhaps the most thoughtless, almost cruel remark he ever made to me, "Are you never going to get over this baby stage? I thought we were ready for some freedom."

Erin was born November 6, 1963. In spite of that thoughtless comment of Bob's, Erin's birth actually brought us closer together. She was indeed a bonus baby.

Because we were so far away, Erin saw far less of either her

Erin goes snorkeling before she's born.

Grandpa Warren and Cleora, or of Bob's parents than the others did during their early childhood. However, Erin (and the others) had Paul and Mabel Johnson who were truly surrogate grandparents.

We met Paul and Mabel briefly when they visited Paul's daughter Nadean when she lived next door to us in West Des Moines.

Bob spent his first weekend in California with Paul and Mabel, and soon after we moved to Buena Park, we all visited them in Fullerton. Our bond with them formed quickly.

We were lucky to have them in our lives for many years.

The letters I wrote during Erin's childhood were different from those in the late 50s. No longer did I focus almost entirely on the children and their escapades. I reported more on my activities, my classes, and on things Bob and I were doing together. These reports are not what this book is about.

For this reason, instead of sharing letters in their entirety, as was the pattern for the 1957-1959 sections of this book, Part IV consists of *excerpts* from letters to my father and his wife Cleora. These excerpts are my attempt to paint a picture of Erin as a little girl just as I've tried to do for Mike, Steve, Pati, and Eric in the preceding pages.

December 19, 1963

Dear Dad and Cleora,

If Erin cooperates, I am settling down with a cup of coffee. I told Pat that after I write to you, I'm going to "visit with" (write a letter to) Lorna Anderson, a friend who moved to Ohio not long ago. Her Scottie is about Pat's age.

"I used to love Scottie," Pat responded nostalgically.

I try not to gush about Erin in letters because I know how dull this can be to other people (but surely not to grandparents). I must tell you one story. Last Sunday night we all went to the church choir program. A nursery was available, but at Christmas I have this sentimental idea that the children all belong with us. Erin (*six weeks old*) was in absolutely no mood to sleep during the entire program, and it was the beautiful-music type so we couldn't let her make a sound if we could possibly prevent it.

She started to fuss early, so Bob handed her to me and whispered, "FEED her." For years, I've fussed about the ridiculousness of the social custom that seems to say a mother can't feed her baby in church if she's nursing. So at last, bright lights, high school boys sitting in front, and all, I fed her. I felt rather exhilarated at finally doing what I felt was right and the only sensible approach. And I really doubt if anyone noticed. A blanket strategically placed made us feel fairly inconspicuous.

Later, I was holding Erin and patting her to keep her quiet while Rosemary Petersen, an extremely talented woman, was giving a Christmas reading about a crippled little boy who went to see the baby Jesus. Erin was quiet for a long time, but suddenly, just as the woman came to the place where the little boy looked at the baby and "the baby cried," guess who did? Sweet

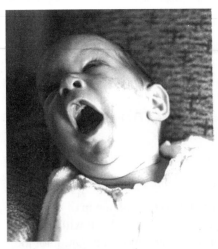

Erin's so-o-o sleepy.

little Erin. Bob wondered if I'd pinched her. After her quite appropriate sound effect, she was quiet again.

She's awfully sweet. She still has her dark hair in her Mohawk hair cut, but is getting bald in front in readiness for blonde hair, no doubt. When she wakes up and stretches, she looks exactly like Pat's Thumbelina doll did last year before the doll's spring broke. I had no idea then that doll was so life-like. I'd forgotten a tremendous amount of such important information as what a baby looks like while stretching.

I just had an idea. As soon as I feed Erin (which I must do NOW, she says), I'm going to decorate her basket with a red ribbon. It's in the living room, and perhaps I can find ornaments to hang around the bottom too. After all, she's one of our more important Christmas decorations this year, don't you think?

I was typing my paper for my anthropology class the night I went into labor with Erin, and life has been rather rushed ever since. The children helped us decorate the tree, the gifts are pretty much done, and everything is fine, except I didn't quite have that special feeling that Christmas usually brings – until a few days ago. It was about midnight and I was sitting in the living room nursing Erin. I looked at her, then over at the tree, and suddenly it hit me. *Christmas is here, and life is good.*

Love, Jeanne

February 26, 1964

Dear Dad and Cleora,

Heather has kittens, but they're not Siamese. She has them only because she got out the broken window in the back door and was gone for 15 minutes one morning before we got up in December. They are sweet, but not as sweet as Erin. Except on Wednesday nights, that is, judging from last week.

Glen Doyle, two houses away, took care of Erin last semester along with the other children, and it looks as if Glen may have Erin again part of the time this spring. Erin has taken a great dislike for the 14-year-old sitter we have. Apparently she cried most of the time last week until Bob got home at 6:15 (I leave at 4), and wasn't even especially hungry. I had thought the only problem was that she doesn't like bottles, but now she eats enough cereal and fruit to get by for that long.

I was convinced she wasn't old enough to care who had her – until Mary (the sitter) came early Friday night. We were going to a friend's for dinner and taking Erin with us. I handed Erin to Mary while I dressed so they could get used to each other. I then discovered sweet little Erin, with whom I've had such great fun this winter, is a mess. I think the term "spoiled" is such a silly one, but I really don't know what else to call it. She cried so hard she spit up. Bob took her, and then she was happy

She adores the other children when we're home, but apparently refuses to let them comfort her when we're gone. So what do we do? Are you perhaps chuckling to yourself about the Lindsays who didn't think they had spoiled children? (Although we had admitted that Eric had had a little too much attention and perhaps his own way too much the past two or three years.) I still

Erin is fine with her siblings – but not the babysitter.

say a 31/2-month-old child has no business caring who has her as long as she's full, warm, dry, and handled lovingly. Erin doesn't agree.

When we take her out with us, she smiles and coos at nearly everyone and has such a ball . . .

On another subject – Lately I've been feeling philosophical – about old age, of all things. I think I'm going through a stage, and am wondering if most people do. I've been looking older, and have found a few gray hairs during the past year. Realizing it was completely ridiculous, I confess I even pulled a few out.

In pictures this year I've noticed many more lines around my eyes, and of course I told myself that after all, I am practically middle aged. I tell myself that every age has its advantages, and I don't mind at all being older. But I didn't really believe it. Suddenly, however, I really don't think I mind. I kind of think I'd like salt-and-pepper hair and am looking forward to it, hoping, however, that when it does come, I'll have the money and time to take proper care of it. With gray hair, I doubt if one can get by with the casual hairstyles one can in one's youth.

Love, Jeanne

April 7, 1964

Dear Dad and Cleora,

We went to the beach yesterday, and it was Erin's first real trip there. She was along when Bob and I went to Laguna Beach with the Morfords a month or two ago, so she'd seen the ocean, but hadn't been down in the sand. She adapted pretty well yesterday, considering that it was quite chilly.

My neighbor, Glen Doyle (who helped deliver Erin) drove us down. Pat was along, too, for she'd been sent home with a stomachache in the morning, and I thought the fresh air and walking might even help her. Apparently constipation was her problem, and she felt better at the beach. Her friends were rather shocked that Pat went to the beach while she was home sick.

I'd never realized how difficult it would be to lug the stroller through the sand. I thought the sand would be too cold to lay Erin on it, and I didn't want to take the playpen until I have a big boy along to carry it. Bob commented later that the sand would ruin the playpen wheels anyway. Alice facetiously suggested taking a sled, and I thought it an excellent idea. We have a very lightweight flying saucer type sled, so maybe I'll try it next time.

Glen's husband is due back Wednesday from seven months at sea. He's a chaplain in the Navy for three years, and this is the first time he's been gone. Glen has had a rather horrible winter. Now she's about to go batty with excitement, and is looking for ways to pass the time until Larry gets here. We may go back down to the beach Friday.

Erin's been waking at 4 a.m. promptly each night, whether I feed her early or late. The other night I decided to let her cry. So I did – 30 minutes the first time, then I fed her. Next night I stretched it to 35 minutes, then got up to feed her, but by then she was back to sleep. Ah-ha, I thought, I'm winning. And I really thought so the next morning when, after crying for about five minutes at 5 a.m., she was silent. (All this time, we'd put her crib in the living room at night.)

At 6 a.m. I got up, thinking I'd wake her to feed her so we could eat our breakfast in peace after she finished. I walked out to the living room – and there were all the children, with Mike sitting on the couch holding Erin and reading! He'd been holding her at least an hour. "I couldn't let her cry," he said.

Aftermath: I explained to Mike what I was trying to do, and now Erin has learned to sleep through nicely. If she wakes about 6, someone is apt to go in and pat her or hold her until I get out there. Somehow that little anecdote is a remarkably accurate example of other happenings in her young life.

She was awake a lot during Easter vacation and wanted much more attention than usual. "Must be her age," I thought.

But the next Monday she slept beautifully most of the day – until just before Eric arrived home at 2:30. She has a marvelously well-built clock within her apparently. It's almost as if she's sleeping as much as possible to conserve her strength when she and I are alone. Then she can be bright and cheerful when

Reluctant mother Heather says, "I didn't choose this!"

her brothers and sister are here.

I've been taking lots of slides of the kittens this week because tomorrow I'm taking them to the pet shop. We've only given one away. They're cute, but the most alley cat looking kittens I've ever seen. Heather often looks at them as if she's saying, "Surely they can't be MINE!"

Erin discovered Heather last night. They've mostly ignored each other, but suddenly when I was holding Erin, and Heather was sitting on the back of the couch about two feet away, Erin started smiling and cooing. Of course I was thrilled, telling Bob to look, etc. After about two minutes of this, Heather very deliberately stood up, turned around, and sat down again with her back to Erin! That cat can be a bit nasty.

Heather is very different from Cleo, her daughter who now lives with Donna Grahek three houses away. Donna has kept Erin several times for an hour or two, and each time Cleo is very eager to get in the room with her, sleeping beside Erin if she can get away with it.

Cleo was in heat the other day, and Kathi (Donna's daughter who is 8) wondered why Cleo wanted kittens so badly. My comment was that she probably thinks her kittens will be like Erin, and what a shock real kittens will be to her!

Sing, the Siamese who fathered Heather's litter last year, was howling outside Donna's door the other day, but she didn't let Cleo out. Kathi commented, "Poor Sing. He probably hasn't gotten to fertilize anybody for a long time."

Friends of Bob's parents (eight of them) came over to meet Erin Saturday. They brought her an adorable outfit. I commented that I liked it so much more than lacy things, and asked how they knew what we'd like. One of the men retorted, "You *should* like it. It took four women four hours to pick it out!"

They took turns holding Erin and talking to her, and also spent time looking at our photo albums. Anyone who will hold my baby and look at our albums is extremely welcome here.

Love, Jeanne

We all, Steve, Eric, Mike, Jeanne, Erin, Pat climb Mt. Waterman. Daddy carried Erin all the way. He also took the photo.

August 11, 1964

Dear Dad and Cleora,

Erin is now eating peanut butter sandwiches. Steve made sandwiches for five or six children a few minutes ago. He dropped one, which Erin caught and started eating. So I've forgotten about blending the cottage cheese and fruit she usually has for lunch. She's filling up on her sandwich and peeled apple, like the rest of the kids. Luckily her hair is about the same color as the peanut butter. If it weren't, it would be now.

November 6, 1964.
A squished up
birthday cake is best.

February 4, 1965

This being home is absolutely glorious, but I don't think I'll mind starting classes next week – an anthropology class Tuesday and Thursday mornings (Erin will stay with Frieda again) and a home economics graduate course Tuesday evenings.

Erin is awfully sweet right now, and really fun to have around. Sometimes after breakfast she comes up and wants me to hold her. Since my plans this week include lots of reading, and it certainly doesn't matter whether this is before dishes are done

Erin, we're not in Iowa anymore.

or after, I sit down on the couch and read. Erin plays happily nearby, frequently coming to crawl over me and be friendly.

Most mornings after her nap, we go outside for a while about noon, and she wanders around playing while I read. She's looking so grown-up now. We firmly intend to take a bunch of photos this weekend.

May 31, 1965

A week ago Saturday we climbed a mountain! Bob decided we could make it if we took it slowly. So we went up Mt. Waterman, and Bob carried Erin all the way. We were all tired when we got home, but it was a lovely day.

We went to the beach yesterday and the day before and had a wonderful time, but now I'm sunburned and stiff. This happens every summer, and I'm sure it will continue.

We took the playpen for Erin, and she surprised us by co-operating beautifully. We stayed five hours yesterday. I learned that by handing Erin a crust of bread at appropriate intervals, she stays reasonably happy for a long time.

Love, Jeanne

December 20, 1965

Dear Dad and Cleora,

Tonight Steve, Pat, Eric and Mike strung popcorn for the Christmas tree, the popcorn they managed not to eat. Popcorn strings add a lot to a Christmas tree, don't they?

Our tree this year is tall, ceiling-high, but quite skinny. We wanted room left for sitting. My favorite "decoration" is Erin's rocking chair in the corner beside the tree with Erin sitting in it.

Incidentally, she can ride her tricycle now, so she's out in the world with the rest of them.

Are you interested in what the children are making this year? Mike is buying gifts with his paper route money but the others still wanted to make things – which is nice AND time consuming. Steve made Eric a wonderful electric toy (with NO help from me). You throw a disc at the box, and if you hit the right place, a light flashes on. I'm really impressed! He made Mike a sharp, very masculine red homespun apron (Mike requested an apron) with bright arrows of different color iron-on tape for decoration. For Pat he made a pink polka dot stuffed doll with a loud flowered dress. Pat wants no dolls or doll clothes this year, but we thought this one looked very teenagerish. I'm sure she'll like it.

Steve had hoped to make Erin a busy box as described in the December *Sunset*, but it's looking too expensive and complicated this 20th day of December. We must decide on something else. I think he's going to make Bob a game, also from *Sunset*.

Eric made his first stuffed animal yesterday, a bright pink-blue-gold-maroon striped lion for Erin with spools for feet. Today I bought bricks that I think he will spray-paint white and

Erin and Mike on Christmas morning

glue felt to the bottom for bookends for the others. If we get to a 31 Flavors ice cream store for cartons, he may cover fresh wastepaper baskets for them too.

Pat made Eric a game, and tomorrow will start the plywood book racks for Mike and Steve. She plans to make a flannel numbers book for Erin, and has embroidered RL on two handkerchiefs for Bob.

If we get it all done, it will be a successful season. All of these gifts will be opened Christmas Eve, in front of the fire after the 7 p.m. candlelight service at church. We'll bring home Shakey's pizza as always for Christmas Eve. Mabel and Paul will spend Christmas with us, as usual.

I'm attempting to make a gift, too, and doing more poorly than the kids. The Arabella and Annie dolls that were on the November cover of *Family Circle* are my goal. Annie is the big doll with several changes of clothes, and Arabella is her little doll. This afternoon, with Steve's help, I stuffed the little one and sewed most of her clothes. I tried to embroider her face, a nice happy one like the picture. Somehow I made her look sad even with her green eyes and a turn-up red mouth! And I didn't want a sad doll for Erin. As for the big one, if I can get one of the outfits made plus the doll, I'll feel successful. Erin's too young to want extra sets of clothes anyhow. There'll be another Christmas.

Love, Jeanne

February 3, 1966

Dear Dad and Cleora,

Speaking of child rearing – I think mothers tend to be absolutely neurotic over toilet-training. I've had perfect strangers tell me in great detail about their child's prowess at the toilet. At the risk of getting a similar reputation with you, I'll tell you what we've been doing the past two days.

First, as past history, I do not understand the term toilet-*training*. It's ridiculous, first because one trains a puppy, not a child. Second, one wears a diaper until one gets tired of it, or as long as someone is willing to pin it on. (Erin has tried unpinning hers without much luck.) Eventually one uses the toilet like other people. In the meantime, one's mother's friends make all sorts of silly comments about diapers such as, "Shouldn't she be wearing panties?" etc.

And one's father, if it's this family, makes cracks about hoping her teacher will understand and be helpful in school. Alice, our Unitarian friend, thinks such things might even fit into Show and Tell time.

To get to the point, we left Pat in charge of Erin during Mike

Erin is a goofy little girl.

Steve takes Erin for a wild ride.

and Steve's piano lessons Tuesday afternoon. It rained a little, and I arrived home to find the laundry I'd hung outside still on the line. I scolded Pat for not bringing that in. Then I noticed Erin without plastic pants, and wearing panties. I was annoyed. Pat apparently was too lazy to put a diaper on her little sister.

Pat informed me that Erin had wet twice in the toilet. So with Pat in charge the rest of the evening and next morning, there were no accidents. I attempted to compose a convincing note to the school asking them please to excuse Pat for a few days so she could toilet-teach her little sister. I didn't succeed in producing a literary masterpiece, so Erin and I have struggled along as best we could for two days – several accidents yesterday, but none today except early this morning when she wet on the dictionary. I mentioned this to Bob when he phoned, and he seemed confused. He'd left the dictionary on the floor by the front window, so it was a perfectly normal phenomenon.

However, goofy little Erin wets about every 15 minutes, and wants me to sit on the bathtub and listen to her chatter each time. I'm pretty tired of exclaiming about the swans on the shower curtain and the boats in the bathtub and the howling cats outside the window all day long. Excuse me, I should say, the "kitty cry-ing." If this keeps up, I'll have to set up my typewriter or sewing machine or something in the bathroom, perhaps in the tub?

Love, Jeanne

August 22, 1967

Dear Dad and Cleora,

We had Erin's hair cut into a pixie last week. She had sort of a bald spot, and I took her to a dermatologist. He gave me some salve for it, and called her condition a long unpronounceable name. He said if it wouldn't be too traumatic, it would be better to cut off her hair. So we did, and she looks awfully cute, better than before, we think. And her hair is growing back in.

We took Erin to the beauty school here to have her hair done, and Bob took a batch of pictures of the process. He mentioned the pictures before she was assigned to an operator, and just as I expected, a pretty little blonde did the cutting, while a very mousey brunette cut mine. Each did an excellent job.

The woman in charge at the beauty school seemed to know much more about Erin's scalp condition than had the derma-

Heather and Erin are great friends now.

tologist. He was quite vague, but this woman briskly asked if Erin had had quite a bit of cradle cap, and I suddenly remembered that she often did. The woman explained what probably happened and why the salve would help. But there's still enough hair there that applying the salve makes an awful mess.

This may sound more important and serious than it is. Erin is not bald, the spot doesn't even show unless you look for it, and I think you'd still claim her for a granddaughter.

Erin loves riding on Eric's shoulders.

Sini arrived last Saturday evening. As I think I told you, she's the German exchange student who will live with us all year. She's 19 months older than Mike, and is a senior at Western.

I think she was feeling pretty uneasy when she got off the plane and met us. Soon after we started driving home, Erin broke the ice.

Sini sneezed, and Erin very clearly said, "Gesundheit!" It's the only German we know. Somewhere, Erin heard someone use this word instead of "God bless you" after a sneeze. It was quite appropriate.

As Sini was going to bed, she came over to me and said, "I think if I'm going to be your daughter for a year, I'll kiss you good night." Of course I was thrilled.

Love, Jeanne

August 28, 1967

Dear Dad and Cleora,

The Graheks moved to Ventura a week ago, and I miss them. It's hard coming home nights and seeing their house all dark and alone, and knowing I can't run over there when I have a few spare minutes.

Do you know what really broke me up Friday? Donna was gone, and Mike Grahek (13) came over to tell us goodbye. After he left, I realized how little I'd said to Erin about them moving. I quickly explained, and suggested she go tell Mike goodbye.

Erin tore down the street yelling, "Mike, wait for me," and finally caught him in front of Lucia's. She grabbed him around the leg, nearly knocking him over, and kissed him. Mike sat down on Lucia's fence to talk to her. And it really hit me. Do you know I've never had a really close friend in the neighborhood leave before? It's always been us who moved on. I miss the Graheks.

October 2, 1967

This was my first morning working at Erin's nursery school, other than the first day when no regular schedule was set up. I'm exhausted! Four-year-olds are much much worse than three-year-olds.

Nursery school teaching is another of the many occupations I firmly intend never to enter. However, one four-year-old is okay. I just went into Pat's room where Erin is sleeping because Mike is in their room with a stomachache. Erin looked so sweet asleep with her books around her. I took a slide photo of her. I tried to take a close-up, but the camera jammed at that moment, or perhaps it's out of film.

Erin loves to visit Steve's bunnies.

Steve is raising rabbits as his 4-H project. The rabbit cage is out by the back fence. Each morning before school, Steve goes out to feed his rabbits. Almost every day he gets Erin on his shoulders and takes her out to "help" him. She loves it.

Pat is studying the Greek myths in seventh grade. Her assignment last week was to illustrate the story of Cupid. At her suggestion, with Erin's enthusiastic approval, I took Erin to Orangeview dressed in panties and a banner across her chest with Cupid written on it in red letters. Erin posing on the teacher's desk was the illustration while Pat did her report. I think both of them were successful in their efforts.

Love, Jeanne

January 7, 1969

Dear Dad and Cleora,

I think kindergarten may be one of the nicest stages. Erin has an excellent teacher, and it's such fun watching how much she enjoys learning. Every day she comes home bubbling about her experiences.

I finally bought her cowboy boots the other day. She'd been wearing red rubber rain boots for months as substitutes. Then all her friends (all boys, of course) got cowboy boots for Christmas, and she wanted them badly. Bob still didn't think she needed them, but for once I decided his superior judgement wasn't valid. Besides, she had nearly enough money in gifts from grandparents.

We foolishly gave Erin a doll for Christmas, plus a truck racetrack. She thoroughly enjoyed both – all day Christmas. It happened to be raining all day which perhaps explains it. Ever since then, she's spent her whole time playing cowboys with the little boys on the block. After all, she's a boy – just ask her!

I was floored the other day at a comment she made, and I wonder if sweet little Erin is more violent than I realize. Mark is a very sturdy, well built little boy across the street, a little younger than she is.

Erin suddenly said to me quite indignantly, and for no apparent reason, "Do you know what Mark's daddy told Mark? He told him that if Erin hit him again, he should hit her back!"

Other mothers in the block complain about Mark's violent tendencies, and I've been pleased all fall to see that he and Erin play together so "nicely." Perhaps I've found the reason.

Soon she'll be riding her two-wheeler.

November 5, 1969

Tomorrow Erin will be six. We're getting her a bicycle. The others didn't have bicycles until they were 7, but she's been riding her friend Eddie's bike for a month now. She's been pleading for one for a number of months. I hope she's mature enough to ride it safely. I think she'll be pleased tomorrow morning when we wheel it into her room.

We're not planning a party for her friends. Instead Eric and I are going to take her to their junior high football game in the afternoon, then have Jacobsons over to share her ice cream and cake. I made her a dress much like Pat's cheerleader outfit from the leftover scraps, and she'll wear it to the game. Of course she's been wanting to go to a game, but until now I was too busy studying to take her.

Erin is reading more and more. She still wears either cowboy boots, jeans and flannel shirt if it's HOT outdoors, and bikini bathing suit pants (no top) if it's COLD outdoors. She's a bit of a nut but very nice.

Love, Jeanne

Afterword
Fifty Years Later

Mike, Eric, Erin, Bob, Jeanne, Steve, Pati Lindsay, circa 2002

Afterword

After eight months of renting, we bought a house in Buena Park. All the children grew up in this house, and continue to come back for holidays and other visits. Instead of moving as we needed more room, we remodeled the house nine times. (I'm addicted to the sound of saws and hammers.)

The four little Lindsays and our bonus baby grew up on schedule. Major mishap, for their parents, at least, was the period of living with four teenagers. Certainly a change from the preschool years. In fact, those teen years were quite traumatic. No longer did we have the All-American family. (I also learned along the way that no one has that perfect family.)

Mike and Steve, especially, rebelled enthusiastically. But everyone made it through, and amazingly, became self-supporting, responsible, and, I think, reasonably happy citizens.

Actually, I worried a little about Erin. *Her* teen years went smoothly. Even clothes shopping – she and her dad shopped together for her clothes, and actually enjoyed it! Not typical, I think, for teen girls.

Then, when Erin was 22, I read *Passages: Predictable Crises of Adult Life* by Gail Sheehy (1984). Sheehy writes that adolescents *need* to rebel. If they don't then, they will later, and that rebellion will be even harder for them.

The next morning at school, I said to Stephanie Winter, with whom I had co-taught for several years, "I'm worried about Erin. Sheehy says she should have rebelled. She hasn't, and I'm concerned she'll have a tough time later."

Stephanie broke into gales of laughter. "Jeanne," she said,

"Erin has rebelled plenty. You just haven't noticed. I've *heard* your stories about her!"

If only the first child could be as easy as the last.

But after we adjusted to their new personas, Mike and Steve were fine too. After skiing through his 20s, Mike started law school at age 30. (He never reached his childhood goal of farming with Grandpa Warren.) Mike is now a partner in a large law firm in Denver. He and Tammy live in Boulder with their two children. Alex is a junior at the University of Colorado, Boulder, and Will is a freshman at Colorado University located in Colorado Springs.

Steve moved to Oklahoma at age 19, with rock band aspirations. Instead, he learned the printing trade, founded Action Printing, and retired in 2006 at age 52. (Steve never became the politician which, when he was 3, I thought might be his destiny.) He and Kathi live on a cliff high above the Pacific in southern Oregon.

Pati worked several years as an accountant, and then developed an interest in the trucking business. She bought her first 18-wheeler when she was 28. She drove cross country by herself for eight years, then with her partner Kent for eight more years. Now Pati focuses on gardening at her home in Eugene, Oregon, as well as managing their business affairs while Kent drives their truck.

A high point in my life was riding across the country twice with Pati in her truck. I discovered that truckers have their own unique culture, and I loved it.

Eric developed great expertise in woodworking. In fact, he built an extensive deck over the ravine in his back yard and that's where he and Kim were married. Now he's general manager of Exova, an analytical chemistry laboratory. He and Kim live in Whittier, California, with their three children. Rachel and Josh will soon graduate from California State University, Fullerton, while Trav recently received an MBA in Entrepreneurship from CSUF.

Erin and Samantha have been together since 1996. They each gave birth to a daughter, Sophie to Erin, and Anneliese to Sam. The girls know David, their biological dad, and frequently see him. All three adults work in research support at Caltech in Pasadena. A high point for the family was Erin and Sam's wedding in July, 2008, during the five months that year in which gay marriage was legal in California.

After eight months with Waste King, Bob started working for Autonetics, which became Rockwell (now Boeing). He remained there for 40 years, then retired. After retirement he had more than a decade of travel and active involvement in community and church activities before he was diagnosed with Alzheimer's Disease. He died at home in March 2005.

My life has more or less divided itself into decades. In the 50s, intensive childrearing. In the 60s I took one or two classes each semester at CSULB, working first for a teaching credential, then graduate school. In the 70s and 80s I taught a teen parent program in Cerritos, California. Since 1977, I have been writing and publishing books and other resources for pregnant and parenting teens.

And what about my father, the recipient of these letters? He lived to see his grandchildren grow up, and to meet all of his great-grandchildren except Sophie and Anneliese. He had 37 years of marriage with Cleora, who died in 1995. Dad lived another five years, and all but the last one or two years were mostly good. He was 107 when he died just two hours before his great-granddaughter Sophie was born.

Our family has been very lucky.

Jeanne Lindsay
December, 2009

About
the Author

Jeanne Lindsay founded Morning Glory Press in 1977. She has published more than forty books plus other resources for pregnant and parenting teens and for those who work with this special population. She authored 21 books, but this is her first title that has nothing to do with teen pregnancy. She has enjoyed her work with teen parents tremendously, but says writing *Four Little Lindsays and How They Grew* was *really* fun.

Jeanne was born on a farm in Kansas, and graduated from Kansas State College (now KSU), Manhattan, Kansas, with a degree in Home Economics and Journalism. In the 60s, she earned a teaching credential and two M.A.s (Home Economics and Anthropology) from CSU, Long Beach. She also earned counseling and administrative credentials.

In 1972, Jeanne founded the Teen Parent Program in the ABC Unified School District, Cerritos, California, and taught there for 16 years.

In addition to the five children described in this book, Jeanne and Bob have seven grandchildren. Jeanne still lives in the house in Buena Park, California, which she and Bob bought in 1960.